THE LITTLE GRAMMAR PEOPLE

The publisher would like to thank the author's children, Tess and Chris Horwitz, for agreeing to bring this book back into print and for their edits to the text.

This revised edition published 2017

By Living Book Press

147 Durren Rd, Jilliby, 2259

Copyright © The Estate of Nuri Mass (1942 and 2017)

National Library of Australia Cataloguing-in-Publication entry:

Creator:	Mass, Nuri, author.
Title:	The Little Grammar People / Nuri Mass ; illustrated by Celeste Mass.
ISBN:	9780648063322 (hardback)
	9780648035619 (paperback)
Target Audience:	For primary school age.
Subjects:	English language--Grammar--Juvenile fiction.
	Adventure Stories
Other Creators/	
Contributors:	Mass, Celeste, illustrator.

Peeping out here and there.

THE LITTLE GRAMMAR PEOPLE

By
NURI MASS

Illustrated by
CELESTE MASS

LIVING BOOK PRESS
2017

I DEDICATE THIS BOOK

TO

MY CHERISHED MOTHER

MY INSPIRATION IN ALL THINGS

ALSO TO

ENGLISH-SPEAKING CHILDREN EVERYWHERE

There is a land of shining flowers,
Of dream-like palaces and towers.
Where little laughing people dwell
By fairy hours.
And oh, the grass is velvet green,
But only very seldom seen,

For mortals do not see or hear
Except with mortal eye and ear,
So witching joys they cannot know,
However near.
No fairy smiles for them or sings:
Theirs is a world of lifeless things.

And so, that pretty land where dwell
The Grammar folk by fairy spell,
And where these little people e'er
Their stories tell,
Can only live for children who
Are sure that magic things are true.
So, with a fairy hand in hand,
Come, let us away to the Grammar Land!

CHAPTER I

A BIG TROUBLE

IT was a very tearful little Linda Robin who stayed back in the school-room one day after her twin brother Barry had packed up his bag and hurried out, with all the other boys and girls of her class, in single file. One by one she watched them as they bade good-bye to Miss Randal and tossed away all the cares and seriousness of the past few hours in their eagerness to get home. Home! First into the arms of a darling bright-eyed mother, then down into the delicious-smelling kitchen to make a merry raid upon such treasures as biscuits and blackberry jam.

Things like that, however, could be the reward for only the good and happy, and as Linda at that moment was feeling the very opposite in every way of good and happy, to think of them made her just a little bit more miserable; and as that little bit more was exactly enough to set free a company of large, rolling tears, out these came tumbling, one by one, chasing each other helter-skelter down her cheeks and splashing over her pretty blue dress.

"Goodness gracious me, Linda!" Miss Randal cried out, looking round and seeing her after the other children had left. "Whatever—Why, come dear, and tell me all about it. I don't really think it can be half as bad as all that."

Linda walked up slowly and placed a confiding hand into

her teacher's kind, comforting one. "It's just that—that I feel such a dunce, Miss Randal," she stammered miserably.

At that her teacher—a tall, sparkling-eyed young woman with a ready smile and a light, bouncing kind of voice-seemed thoroughly surprised. "A dunce?" she repeated. "Why dear me, it's quite the other way about. You're one of my very best pupils. Didn't you know that? Except, of course," she added teasingly, "where grammar is concerned—"

"Yes, yes," Linda broke in, with a tiny catch in her throat that sounded very much like a sob, "that's it, Miss Randal: that—that nasty—awful—horrid grammar, those mean little parts of speech, that—"

"Hush, dear, hush!" Miss Randal exclaimed, looking shocked and alarmed. "What a silly little girl you are to talk like that, Linda! How could you expect to be welcomed or to be able to hold your own in the Kingdom of Grammar if you approach it like that, growling and scowling and calling it names? And just how friendly do you think the Parts of Speech can feel towards any one who calls them mean? How would you feel yourself? Dear me, Linda, you really will have to be more careful from now on how you behave in that good old Kingdom of Grammar."

It was now Linda's turn to look astonished, and, with wide-open eyes and suddenly halting tears, she did so to perfection. "The—the Kingdom of Grammar?" she said, almost in a whisper.

"Yes." And Miss Randal laughed outright. "But for goodness' sake, dear, don't look so afraid of it."

"Oh," cried Linda, "but I *am* afraid of it. Wherever it is, it must be the very worst and horridest place, packed full of—oh, cannibals and hobgoblins and—" Here words failed her completely, and in any case the twinkle in Miss Randal's eyes did not encourage her to continue in this quarrelsome strain, so she merely looked down at her toes and was silent.

Then Miss Randal gave her hand a tiny squeeze and, with a voice grown suddenly softer and deeper as though filled with secret excitement, she said, "You're really very much mistaken there. dear. But even if you weren't—even if Grammar Land were filled with cannibals and hobgoblins—just think what

Cannibals and hobgoblins.

fun and adventure you could have there! In fact, Linda, the more I think of it the more I envy you. There are lots and lots of things I'd give to be in the shoes of such a lucky little girl as you. Fancy having a real live trip to the Kingdom of Grammar in store!"

"Oh, but I haven't got that, Miss Randal," Linda protested with a puzzled expression. "I—I wouldn't even know the first thing about how to get there—that is, even supposing I—"

"Oh, but you would, Linda, for, in spite of what you were about to say just now, you do want to visit the Kingdom of Grammar. I know you do. Think what fun it would be to meet the Parts of Speech in person and to be able to tell them exactly what you thought of them—that is, if you weren't being kept too busy listening to what they thought of you!"

By this time an eager smile was shining somewhere on Linda's face, but her eyes were still a wee bit sombre with doubt and puzzlement. "Oh yes. Miss Randal, that would be ever so wonderful, and it really would be the best fun in the world to go there, but—" and here her voice sank to a trembling little whisper, "how could I—we—Barry and I—how could we ever get there?"

"Dear me!" Miss Randal exclaimed. "That's the easiest question of all to answer, for with Desire as your guide you won't need to think twice about it. Desire, you see, can solve even the hardest problems, and knows off by heart the way to every place there is."

"But—but where is he himself to begin with?"

"Why, he's right inside you—in your own heart," Miss Randal explained. Then, suddenly bursting into a merry laugh and smoothing away a wisp of hair from the small girl's forehead, she added, "Now, you run along home, dear, and have a good talk to Barry about it, and by to-morrow—why, goodness only knows what might happen between now and to-morrow!"

CHAPTER II

THE ADVENTURE BEGINS

IT was to a tiny school somewhere near the heart of the Australian bush that Linda and Barry went every day, and between it and home there was a darling little woodland creek bordered with wild violets and ferns. Here the children would

A darling little woodland creek.

often stop to play for a few minutes, setting light twigs and pointed gum leaves afloat on the tiny ripples and watching these fairy boats until they were carried far, far away out of sight to goodness knows where. It was always such fun trying to imagine where they might come to rest at last and what strange wee people might be waiting there to welcome them; but neither Barry nor Linda ever followed along the bank beside them to find out, for it was a thousand times better to guess about things than to be quite sure of them.

Here it was, then, that on this particular day Barry was amusing himself playing about with one thing and another while he waited for Linda, and when he saw her little blue-clad figure hurrying towards him through the trees he called out a cheery greeting. "Hullo, Lin! Where've you been?"

"Back at school."

"Heavens, whatever for?"

"Oh, just to have a talk with Miss Randal," Linda replied carelessly, "—about grammar," she added mysteriously.

"Ugh!" Barry. with a wry face and a grunt of disgust, turned on his heel, and was just about to take himself home rather more quickly than usual when he stopped at the sound of Linda's chuckle.

"That's what I thought, too, at first," she said.

And then followed a rapid account of all that Linda and Miss Randal had talked about in the school-room, with, of course, a few extra touches just by way of added persuasion; and by the time this was finished Barry was every bit as keen as Linda to set out on the exciting voyage to Grammar Land. But, with all the eagerness in the world, it still seemed impossible that their wish could ever be granted, and, much as they tried to imagine the Kingdom of Grammar and longed to visit it, there they still were, sitting on the banks of their old familiar creek, with nothing more wonderful around them than ferns, wild flowers and hosts of fallen gum leaves. And although the afternoon sun struck down upon the ground and creek in splashes of rich gold, and although an occasional bird trilled out a short, sweet song and there were peace and beauty everywhere, still at this moment neither Barry nor Linda desired anything so much as to find themselves suddenly far, far away from that lovely spot, peeping and probing into every secret nook in Grammar Land.

"There's my boat!" Linda cried abruptly, throwing an extra large leaf on to the ripples that happened to be passing by at that moment. "And I wish-oh, I wish, I wish—it would take me to the Kingdom of Grammar!"

"Me too!" said Barry, watching to see what course the little boat would take.

And then something very wonderful happened, something that Barry and Linda will never forget. Even when they are an old, old man and woman they will remember it as one of the strangest things in their lives. First of all, the leaf had not gone any distance when it stuck against a clump of reeds and refused to move any farther.

"Well," said Barry, "that is a long and daring journey, I must say!" And, with a long stick, he tried to jerk it out into mid-stream again. But the leaf seemed to have a mind of its own, and the more Barry teased and worried it the more obstinate it grew, swivelling back against the reeds again and again until Barry was quite annoyed with it.

"That's how much it means to take us to the Kingdom of Grammar!" he declared, giving it a really vicious poke this time, of which it took no notice whatever. "What's the matter with the jolly thing?" he snapped, and started to look round for something that *would* send it about its business when suddenly Linda jumped up and plucked him by the sleeve.

"Look, Barry, look!" she cried, her voice trembling a little. "The—the leaf! It's—oh, Barry!" And then, being a lot too puzzled and a little too frightened to say any more, she merely stood there, clinging to her brother's sleeve and staring at the wilful leaf. And Barry also stood there quite still, staring. And when, after a few seconds, they both looked into each other's eyes, they did so with awe and wonder, for—there was no doubt or dreaming about it—that leaf was certainly growing larger. Slowly, slowly it grew, stretching itself out all over as if it were made of elastic, and letting its sides and ends curl upward at the same time, until there, rocking gently to and fro against a great clump of bulrushes in—why, not in a tiny creek any longer, but in a wide, blue river—was the sweetest sort of boat imaginable, exactly large enough to hold both Linda and Barry.

Neither of the children could say a single word, or even move. But when suddenly a tiny fairy man appeared from nowhere and stood at one end of the boat in a careless and easy manner, his foot perched up on the edge, they both jumped very nearly out of their skins, and Linda, with a little cry of terror, seemed about to run away, when

"Come, come, Lin!" the wee man said in a friendly fashion, throwing back his head and laughing mischievously. "That's surely not the way you're going to welcome me. You shouldn't be afraid of your own Desire when you come face to face with him."

"My—my Desire!" she stammered.

"Yes, yours and Barry's. I've come to take you to the Grammar Kingdom—don't you remember?—where all the Parts of Speech live, and hosts of other people. I'll introduce

Suddenly a tiny fairy man appeared.

you to them, and show you the Palace of Parsing and the Temple of Analysis. Why, I may even introduce you to the mighty king himself."

"Barry," whispered Linda, "are we asleep?"

The little man laughed again—a long, merry laugh. "Come! Into my boat!" he exclaimed. "Don't you think I made it well? And quickly too? And all out of a dead old gum leaf, and even despite your vexing interference, young Barry! Ah yes, a wonderful man is Desire!"

Barry now took a step forward and bowed politely. "Sir Desire, you're certainly very kind, and we do want ever so much to go with you," he said. "But—but I really think we ought to tell mother and father about it first, case they worry. So could you wait for us a minute?"

"No!" came the sharp reply, which made Barry and Linda jump all over again. "Because," their tiny friend explained in his high, shrill voice, "there is no need. We shall be going by fairy time. We are going by it now, although you haven't noticed any difference."

"And what *is* the difference?" asked Linda.

"A minute in mortal time is the same as a day in fairy time, that's all. So that, although by fairy time we're off now on a two days' excursion, you'll be back safe and sound on this shore again within two minutes of mortal time. It's easy, isn't it?"

"Oh yes!" cried the twins together. "Yes, yes, yes!" And, without wasting another second, Barry helped Linda across into the magic boat, then stepped in himself.

When they were both settled comfortably the little man clapped his hands—that was all—and the boat, moving away from the bulrushes, began its long journey down the river.

And very soon it was far beyond any place that either of the children had ever seen.

As they travelled on farther and farther, the banks of the river became more and more beautiful, with a misty, impish kind of beauty, until they looked like Fairyland itself.

"You didn't think the way to Grammar Kingdom was anything like this, did you, children?" said the little man, glancing merrily at each of them.

"Indeed no," replied Linda. "But Sir Desire," she added, a wee bit troubled, "before we started you said something about the king of Grammar Land. Is he kindly? Do you think he'll like us?"

"Oh yes, very kindly. Dear old King Speech! Of course he'll like you—and overlook all the horrid things you've said about his loving subjects the Parts of Speech, too, no doubt."

"I hope he does!" cried Barry with real feeling. "Sir Desire, is he very old?"

"Yes, very old. But he never wears out, as mortal kings."

"Is that what mortal kings do?" Linda looked puzzled.

"Of course. They wear out and you have to get new ones, and sooner or later the new ones wear out too, and so on. Now, King Speech often gets a bit frayed round the edges, owing to the dreadful way people use him at times, but somehow or other he always manages to get mended—and embroidered too, now and then."

By this time their boat had drifted up on to a shore of purest white sand. Sir Desire, springing out, bade the children do likewise, and they did not lose a minute in obeying him. Tense and excited, their hearts jumping up and down in a dozen different places at once, they followed eagerly upon his heels, and soon found themselves at the mouth of a large, dark cave.

Then, turning round and facing the two children while vigorously throwing out his arm towards the mysterious entrance, "Welcome to the Kingdom of Grammar!" the little man cried aloud, with his usual merry laugh.

"Welcome to the Kingdom of Grammar!"

CHAPTER III

MISS NOUN

THEN suddenly he dipped right into the cave, and disappeared so completely in the darkness that Barry and Linda feared they might have lost him, but they quickly sprang in after him and, although they could see nothing of him, they were immediately reassured by the sound of his cheery voice.

"It's rather dark just here," he called out, "but we'll soon be getting out into some light. Be careful of these steps, now, because they're a little uneven, and it would never do for you to fall into the garden of the Parts of Speech head first. You'd only frighten them all away like that. If you approach them quietly and carefully, you'll get on ever so much better with them."

"All right," Linda replied with a slight tremor in her voice. "I'll be careful."

And Barry added a little grunt that sounded very wise and approving.

After a moment's silence Sir Desire's voice again rang out through the cavern. "Many people," he said, "lose track of me altogether in this dark piece of the journey. After trying a few steps they complain that it's far too hard and gloomy, and an awful lot of trouble for nothing. So they simply turn back and go home, and then blame the poor little Parts of Speech for all their difficulties—just imagine that!—before they've even given themselves the pleasure of meeting them."

"I think he means us, Lin, don't you?" Barry whispered.

"I believe he does," was the hushed reply.

Now, for the first time, there was a corner to turn. Sir Desire turned it quickly and the twins, still following closely, were surprised to find themselves suddenly in broad sunlight, the same as that of the ordinary everyday world, and in a most glorious garden. The short grass, all over which were thousands of tiny flowers, was shaded by huge spreading trees, but the golden sunshine was peeping through in countless different shapes and places, and it really looked as if the patterns of light and shade in that garden had been woven by fairy hands.

"Oh, lovely, lovely!" cried Linda. "Dear Sir Desire, please tell us, who lives here in this simply wonderful place?"

Her eyes were sparkling with admiration, and so were Barry's, but the sparkles in the eyes of Sir Desire were even brighter while he answered, in triumph, "Why, can't you guess? The Parts of Speech, of course—Miss Noun, Madam Adjective, Sir Pronoun, Master Verb—"

"Oh, oh," interrupted the small girl, "please show them to us, Sir Desire. Oh, please, please! All of them, one by one. Could we—oh, do you think we could start with Miss Noun, Sir Desire?"

"Certainly," said the little man proudly. "You give me enough power to do anything you wish. I'll bring her straight away."

And with this, he put one hand up to his mouth and called a long, clear note which sounded exactly like a horn in a forest. And that very second there came running up towards Linda and Barry the daintiest little girl imaginable, in a bright yellow frock, who seemed far too tiny a thing to be such an important personage.

He called a long, clear note.

Miss Noun

She curtsied prettily for the two children, and Barry, feeling that this was a good opportunity to prove himself a gentleman, swept off his cap, bowed low, and said, "We're very pleased to meet you, Miss Noun."

"Well, well," she replied, "I'm glad to hear you say that at last. You've taken a frightfully long time about it. I couldn't say how often I've tried to introduce myself to you both, only to have you turn away quite rudely without glancing at me and remark, 'Horrid thing!' "

"Oh," cried Linda solemnly, "we had no idea we were doing anything like that, Miss Noun. I'm sure we wouldn't have offended you for all the world, if only—"

"Dear me," broke in Miss Noun, smiling, "nobody in the Kingdom of Grammar ever gets offended, Linda. We only get sorry, sometimes."

And now a broad smile started playing tricks with Barry's seriousness as he watched this bright, graceful little person whom he had spent so many of his schooldays hating diligently, and, with a chuckle of delight, he exclaimed, "So you're one of those awful nouns!"

"Well, yes and no," she answered doubtfully. "I mean to say that, speaking more correctly, I'm not *a* noun, but Noun itself." And, as that seemed to puzzle both the children quite a lot, she continued, "You see, I, as Noun, am really everything you ever give a name to— everything at once—book, school, table, herd, sideboard, sky, rocks, king, queen, country—"

"But," Linda interrupted, "I don't see you as any of these things. You just look like a tiny little girl to me."

"Not a noun, but
Noun itself.""

"Ah yes, but that is only the form I've chosen to meet you in. Whenever human visitors come to see me—which is very seldom—I appear to them like this, because that makes it so much easier for us to understand each other. However, I could have come to you in quite a different form if I'd liked—as a pair of fire-tongs, for instance, a window, a carpet, or a cloud—because all of these things are nouns. And they are nouns *because* they are things."

"And is that all there is to know about nouns?" asked Barry, looking most surprised.

"Well no, not quite all, Barry," she answered, "but that's the main part. You see, I am a person of a number of different capabilities and moods. I'm not always the same."

"You are always a noun, though," said Linda.

"Yes, just the same as you are always a girl. But that doesn't mean that you and I can't change our moods sometimes. You may be in a happy mood one minute and in an angry one the next, and so on."

"I don't think you are ever angry," Barry objected.

"Perhaps not, but I'm often in a collecting mood."

Linda seemed to think this very funny. "And whatever does that feel like?" she asked, laughing.

"Just as if you want to collect together a whole lot of things that are alike in some way, and give all of them only one name between them. This may seem a queer sort of mood to you, but it's quite natural to me, and when I'm feeling like that mortals call me a 'collective noun'."

"Well!" said Barry. "I never thought collective nouns were so easy."

The tiny girl smiled happily and continued, "Sometimes I feel as if I want to collect a whole lot of people together and call them a 'crowd'—"

Miss Noun

"I call them a 'flock'."

"Then 'crowd' would be a collective noun," Linda interrupted.

"Exactly. When I collect a number of birds together I call them a 'flock', and a number of cattle a 'herd'."

"Then 'flock' and 'herd' would also be collective nouns," said Barry. "And now, Miss Noun, please tell us all about the other moods you have."

"Well," she quickly replied, "sometimes I feel very abstract."

"Absent-minded?" Linda suggested.

"No, no, nothing like that. Let us say, very untouchable."

"That's funny," said Barry.

"Yes, I know. But all the same, I feel that way quite often—you know, just as if nobody could see or hear or touch me, and yet as if I'm there just the same. Sometimes, you see, I feel like freedom or happiness or regret. I do not feel happy or regretful. but simply like happiness itself."

"Yes, I think I understand," said Linda.

"And when this is the way I feel, mortals call me an 'abstract noun'."

"So that 'happiness' is an abstract noun," said Barry, "and 'regret' is another, and 'joy' another, and—Oh, there are any and any amount of them, Miss Noun. You must feel abstract very often."

"I do," she agreed.

"And what about common and proper nouns? How do they come about?" asked Linda.

"Oh, those are what I call my lazy and energetic moods," she replied. "When I am a city and am in a lazy mood, I just say

17

I'm a 'city', and that's all about it. Mortals then call 'city' a 'common noun', because it is the name *common* to every example of that kind of thing. But when I am more energetic, I realize that each separate city is something all to itself, and that there isn't another in the whole world exactly like it, so I get busy and give it a name all its own. I call it 'London', or 'Sydney', or 'Madrid'—whichever one it happens to be—and people then say that 'London' is a 'proper noun'."

"I see," said Linda. "But why should it be called 'proper' just because it belongs to one city only? That seems a funny name to give it."

"Well, Linda," the tiny girl answered, putting her head on one side and smiling as brightly as a sunbeam, "little ladies as young as you can't expect to know everything. But when you're a few years older you might learn something about Latin, and then you'll know that your word 'proper' has been borrowed from a Latin word which means 'belonging to'."

"Latin must be a kind language to lend us one of its words." Barry remarked. "And so, Miss Noun, 'Barry Robin' would be two proper nouns, and 'Linda Robin' would be two more—wouldn't they?—because those names *belong* to us as our very own."

"Right!" said Miss Noun.

Then she, Sir Desire, Linda and Barry all laughed joyously at the same moment, for everything seemed so beautifully simple, and they found one another such very good company.

"I had no idea," said Linda, "that nouns were so easy—and neither had Barry. And it's just ever so nice to have you for a friend, dear Miss Noun."

At that, the little lady looked very happy, and said how glad she was that Linda and Barry did at last think of her as a friend. "And now," she finished, "as I have nothing more to tell you, I shall call Sir Pronoun to come and see you. I really don't know what I'd do without Sir Pronoun. But there! mustn't say any more. I must leave him to tell you all abou that himself. Oh, but just before I go I must recite my own little rhyme to you. It may help you to remember how easy it is to recognize a noun whenever you see one:

> "Chimney, Europe, sadness, flock,
> Mountain, ocean, Venus, town,
> Mary, sympathy and frock—
> Every one of them a noun!"

"Oh, thank you!" said the two children.

"Just repeat it over to yourselves, now," added the tiny girl, "and try to pick out which are the common, proper, abstract and collective nouns in it."

And neither of the twins had a chance to promise her that they would do this, or even to say one more thank you, for little Miss Noun had suddenly disappeared.

CHAPTER IV

SIR PRONOUN

SHE had only been gone a very short while, however, when there came walking towards the twins a rather long, thin boy. His face was so pale and his steps were so slow that Linda could not help asking him if he were sad or worried about anything.

"Oh no," he replied, smiling. "I'm thinking, that's all. You see, I have so much to think about, being Pronoun."

"Yes, I suppose you have," Barry agreed. "Whenever I've been asked a question about you I've had to think a great deal too."

This seemed to amuse Sir Pronoun, for he laughed merrily, crossing and uncrossing his very long legs several times as if he did not know quite what to do with them. "Yes," he continued, "my whole life is one of deep thought, because, as you can tell by my name, I have to stand in the place of Miss Noun."

"Whatever do you mean?" asked Linda, puzzled. "Doesn't Miss Noun stand in her own place?"

"Oh yes, certainly. Sometimes she does, but not always. You must remember that she leads a very busy life and has to be in an awful number of parts at once, and it's my business to help her whenever I can."

A rather long, thin boy.

Sir Pronoun

"That's interesting," said Barry.

"Let me explain myself more clearly," Sir Pronoun went on. "When Miss Noun is needed in a sentence she makes quite sure she is there to begin with, but hops away again like quick-silver, partly because she has so much to do and partly because she's afraid people may grow tired of her. I then step along and say, 'Ladies and gentlemen, with your kind permission, I shall represent Miss Noun for a short time, as she was afraid of tiring you and has gone.' Sometimes I am greeted quite amiably, but other times everybody gets very annoyed, says I

Thrown out of the sentence.

don't make myself at all clear and throws me out of the sentence. Miss Noun then, realizing the situation, appears again in person, and all is well—although, I must admit—" he added dolefully, then paused.

"—that all isn't as well as it might be with you," Linda suggested.

"Exactly," he replied. And he looked so downcast that neither Barry nor Linda had the heart to laugh out loudly, so, for the moment at least, they tucked their laughs away cosily inside themselves.

"But Sir Pronoun, just why is it that you have to think so much?" Barry asked.

"Because," the long boy explained, "Miss Noun is so terribly changeable, and as I have to take her place I must be changeable too. I'm positively the whole time trying to decide whether I should now be a 'personal', 'demonstrative', 'relative' or 'interrogative' pronoun."

"I'm sure that would puzzle me a good bit too," said Barry.

"Although I'd think it easy enough to be personal, at any rate."

Sir Pronoun laughed heartily at this, and then said, "No, no, Barry, you don't understand. The word 'person' doesn't mean the same in Grammar Kingdom as it does amongst mortals. In your world 'person' only means a human, like yourself, but here it can also mean an animal, or a thing."

"Oh, but how?" Linda asked, frowning.

"Just like this. In Grammar Kingdom there are three types of person, and to distinguish them we call them 'first', 'second' and 'third'."

"And what does each one mean?" Barry asked eagerly.

"Well now, wait a minute. young man. I was just coming to that. The one who is actually speaking at the time—we think him the most important, so we call him 'first person'."

"But," Linda objected, "only people can talk, so the word 'person' must be the same in Grammar Kingdom as it is in our world after all."

Sir Pronoun looked slightly peeved. "Not a bit of it!" he said curtly. "You should listen to everything I have to say before you argue the point, young lady. I was just going to add that the one or *thing* being spoken to we think the second most important, or 'second person'. And the one or *thing* being spoken about we think the least important, so we call him, her or it 'third person'."

"Oh, I see," said Barry. "So that I, because I am speaking now, am most important. Therefore I am first person."

"That's what I am," corrected Sir Pronoun.

Barry was shocked. Fancy contradicting just like that, for the sake of it! "What *I* am," he repeated firmly.

Sir Pronoun laughed. "Dear me," he said, "what a lot of explaining you children seem to need! What I meant was that the actual word 'I' is what I am myself, namely a pronoun."

"But you would call it 'first person', wouldn't you?" Barry insisted.

"Yes, certainly."

"So that 'I' is a first personal pronoun. That seems easy enough. And, being a pronoun, it must stand for a noun. Now, what is that noun?"

"Why, 'Barry', of course. That's your own name, isn't it?"

"Yes, yes," said Barry eagerly. "And that's a proper noun, because it belongs to me only."

"And the word 'you' would be a second personal pronoun, wouldn't it? Because it stands for the one or thing being spoken to," said Linda.

"Quite right," replied Sir Pronoun. "You'll find, as you go on thinking, that there are any amount of occasions on which I am 'personal'."

"And then, what about third personal pronouns?" asked Barry. "They would be 'they', 'them', 'their', 'him', 'it', 'she', 'he'—oh, lots and lots of them—as those stand for the things or people being spoken about. How easy it is after all, isn't it, Lin?"

"Yes, very easy. But there are still lots of things I want to ask. For instance, Sir Pronoun, you said a while ago that you were sometimes a relative. Whose relative would that be?"

At this, Sir Pronoun burst into a real fit of laughter, and it was quite a long time before he could stop. "Oh dear!" he cried at last. "You do say some funny things, you two. I'm not *a* relative by any means. I'm just relative."

"Oh," said Barry, doubtfully.

"Yes, I know it sounds like a riddle just now. Small humans mostly take an awful time to understand the doings of

Running between the beginning and end of the sentence.

Grammar folk. Well, I've already told you how Miss Noun has the habit of disappearing as quickly as she appears. But sometimes, when there's quite a lot being said about her, she grows even shyer than usual. This means that I have a frightful amount of work to do, running backwards and forwards between the beginning and end of the sentence, connecting or *relating* things to one another which would otherwise be all higgledy-piggledy."

"Oh, so it's when you are relating things that humans call you a 'relative pronoun'. Is that it?" cried Linda.

"Exactly. Now I shall give you an example of the hard work

Sir Pronoun

I have to do when Miss Noun is extra-specially shy. Just look at this sentence: 'She is the girl who was late for school yesterday.' I appear twice there."

Linda could not help clapping her hands for joy. "Yes, yes," she exclaimed. " 'She' is you—a personal pronoun."

"A third personal pronoun," Barry added.

"Right. And then I appear again a little farther on as 'who'. But when I am 'who' I am a different kind of pronoun altogether. I am a relative pronoun, because—Do you know why?"

"I'm not quite sure," said Barry.

"Well, because I am connecting or *relating* 'she' with what is being said about her, namely that she was late for school yesterday. And look at Miss Noun there, as 'girl'! She knew something else was going to be said about her soon, so she ran off in double quick time. That meant that, if the sentence was to be made in any way clear. I would have to appear in it twice—a very trying business, I can assure you."

"Yes, indeed," Linda agreed. "No wonder you have so much to think about."

"You said, though," continued Barry, eager to know all there was to be known about Sir Pronoun, "that you are sometimes 'demonstrative'. Would that be when you are demonstrating things?"

"We-ell," he replied hesitantly, "when I am *pointing* at things."

"Humans are not allowed to point," said Linda.

"Ah, but they do all the same," said Sir Pronoun. "If they don't point with their fingers, they do with their voices."

"How?" Barry inquired.

"Simply like this. When someone asks you, 'Do you want this?' you may answer. 'No, I want that.' And what are you doing then but pointing with your voice? And what am I doing then but coming to help you do so, as 'that'?"

"Yes, of course. I see now," both children cried out together.

"You must think we're dreadfully inquisitive," Linda remarked, "asking you all these questions, but—"

"Not at all," he replied. "I am often inquisitive too. Sometimes I ask ever so many questions. And it's then that humans call me 'interrogative'."

"That's very interesting indeed," said Barry. "And do you know what? I do believe I can tell you what words you are when you are interrogative."

"Let me see, then!" And Sir Pronoun smiled all over, for he loved to be thought about and taken notice of.

"You are 'which?', 'what?'—"

"And 'who?' " Linda interrupted, "and 'whom?'—"

"Quite right." said Sir Pronoun. And then, suddenly, he added, "Somehow or other, I don't think you and I will ever be bad friends again, because, you see, we understand each other so much better now, and that makes all the difference. Goodbye!"

And with this, Sir Pronoun swung round on his long, thin legs until he was facing in the opposite direction, and, with great, thoughtful steps, he walked slowly away.

CHAPTER V

MADAM ADJECTIVE

WHEN Sir Pronoun was no longer to be seen, Linda looked down at the funny little man beside her. *"Oh, Sir Desire," she said, "this is lovely, lovely!"

"It is that," Barry agreed. "And now, what will happen next, I wonder? Which Part of Speech comes next?"

"I think," Sir Desire announced, looking hugely pleased with himself, "that I'll take you along to the bower of Madam Adjective. I'm sure you'll like to meet her. Ah yes! She's a character all to herself, is Madam Adjective."

"And—and can we go right now?" asked Linda, far too excited even to pretend that she had any patience.

"Yes, indeed!" the little fellow replied airily. And the three set out together towards one end of the garden where there was a tiny rustic gate. Sir Desire opened this and led the way through. "Of course," he said, "Madam Adjective is a wee bit abrupt at times, but you'll just have to take no notice of that. I think you'll like her, all right. We'll soon see, anyway."

"Well," Barry remarked, "since I've grown to like Sir Pronoun I'm quite ready to like anything. Nothing seems nearly as awful now as it did before."

By this time, they had entered a large and very lovely bower formed by trees with tangling branches, and filled with hosts of showery palms and ferns. At one end of it Barry and Linda noticed that the twining creepers had woven themselves into

the form of a perfect swinging couch quite large enough to hold both the mortal children, and Sir Desire as well. But only one fairy-sized person occupied it, and that was Madam Adjective herself.

As the little trio entered the bower she raised her lorgnette in a critical manner, and did not say a word, but merely watched.

Barry and Linda thought she looked an elderly lady, for she had the corners of her mouth turned down.

She raised her lorgnette in a critical manner.

"Do you think she likes us, Barry?" Linda asked rather anxiously.

"I'm not quite sure," he replied.

"That's just her way. you know," Sir Desire murmured hopefully.

"Don't whisper, there!" the stiff lady herself cried out suddenly. "I do not like whispering. Do you—any of you—see anything so very peculiar about me?"

"N-no," Barry stammered, "nothing at all, madam. I think we were only wondering why you should look so cross when you've got such a pretty place to live in."

"Oh! . . . Well," she continued, dropping her lorgnette and smiling pleasantly, "I don't look cross always, you see, but I do quite often. I can, however, be the most amiable of all the Parts of Speech when I wish—the most kindly too, often the most flattering."

"It's rather a pity," said Linda, "that you're not always kindly, don't you think, Madam Adjective?"

"Perhaps you're right," she replied, "but that doesn't alter the fact that my nature is otherwise. I know Miss Noun and Sir Pronoun have already told you how changeable they are, yet I may assure you that neither of them can possibly compete with me in that regard, for I'm seldom more than five minutes in the same mood."

"Goodness!" said Barry. "How very confusing!"

"How very entertaining!" she corrected hastily. "It isn't every Part of Speech that can be scornful one minute, praising the next and angry the next, then indifferent perhaps, then hating, and then loving."

"No indeed," Linda agreed, "I don't suppose it is. Can you really be all that?"

"Well, of course I can—and many other things as well, which you haven't got time to listen to or I to tell you of."

Barry now stepped forward and said politely, "Madam Adjective, could I please ask you a question about yourself?"

"Yes, yes, yes. What is it?" she replied, rapping out her words as though she were a little hammer.

"Well, they say at school that you are often compared, and I'd like to know what with."

"You funny child!" she said, and laughed shortly. Then, stiffening again, she added, "I am to be compared with no one. But I'll explain to you what they mean. It is not that I *am* compared. It is that I compare. I often take a whole lot of things of the same type and arrange them out before me. Then, having decided that they are all—perhaps rather small, I very carefully *compare* their smallness and divide them off into three sections. Those in the first section I label 'small', those in the second 'smaller', and those in the third 'smallest'. And if they are ugly I compare their ugliness in the same way, and also if they are pretty-and so on."

"Oh, I understand," said Linda. "And Madam Adjective, do you like comparing?"

"Very much indeed. Else why do you suppose I'd do it so often? And humans give me two quite interesting names for it, also. When I say the thing—whatever it is—is 'smaller' they call me 'comparative', and when I say it is 'smallest'. they call me 'superlative'. Sometimes, when I am feeling extra enthusiastic about something, I keep on being superlative for a long time. But I've found that humans don't like this sort of thing very much, so for the sake of courtesy I try to hide my real feelings, and become either comparative or merely positive."

"What does it mean when you are 'positive'?" Barry asked.

"Oh, didn't I tell you that? Well, humans call me 'positive' when I say, simply, that the thing is 'small', or 'ugly', or 'pretty'. That's all it means. You know," she hurried on, "I believe you children were rather put about, when you came here first, by the sight of my lorgnette. But I think you understand better now that I simply have to carry it about with me always if I'm going to be able to criticize Miss Noun and Sir Pronoun accurately enough. And it's the main part of my work to criticize. Ah yes, and very interesting it is, too."

"But do you only criticize Miss Noun and Sir Pronoun?" asked Linda.

"Dear me, yes. And that's plenty, I can tell you. I never bother about the other Parts of Speech at all."

"I see. And don't Miss Noun and Sir Pronoun ever object?"

"Sometimes they do, a good deal. But other times I praise them so highly that they forgive me for anything I might have said before, and think themselves mighty lucky that I give them so much attention."

"Of course, I know it's quite natural to you and that you don't mind it," said Barry, "but I know that, for my part, I'd hate to be criticizing for evermore."

"And who said I criticized for evermore?" demanded the wee lady. "On the contrary, my young friend, a description doesn't need to be a criticism, and actually what I'm always doing is describing things in one way or another. And now I'll tell you something else. Often I'm very much like Sir Pronoun in that I simply point out. But, unlike Sir Pronoun, I point out Miss Noun. I don't take her place. In fact, usually she stands right beside me in the sentence."

"And when you are pointing out, Madam Adjective, do humans call you 'demonstrative' also?"

"They do. When they speak or write a sentence such as 'That book is better than this one', I appear three times—once as comparative and twice as demonstrative."

"Yes, 'that' and 'this' are demonstrative and 'better', of course, is comparative. Is that right?" Barry asked eagerly.

"Quite right. And now I want to ask *you* a question. I've been kept busy answering quite long enough. What Part of Speech do you think you are using when you speak of 'two' books, or 'eleven' apples, or the 'third' class?"

Both the children were quite silent for a short time, and then Linda replied slowly, "I think we'd be using you, madam, because 'books', 'apples' and 'class' are all nouns, and 'two', 'eleven' and 'third' describe them in a way. And as you describe things, I should think 'two', 'eleven' and 'third' would all be you."

Madame Adjective seemed delighted with this answer, for she smiled broadly and said, "Right, Linda. You're a very good little thinker. But now, I don't suppose either of you could tell me what name I am given when I am 'two', 'eleven' and 'third'?"

"Again there was silence—a longer one than the last. But finally Barry looked up with a bright sparkle in his eyes. "I know!" he exclaimed. "I remember hearing it once or twice, and now I know what it means. When you are those words—which are all numbers—you must be feeling in a very numeral state of mind, and so you are called 'numeral adjective'."

"Well, well!" she cried. "This, I must say, is far more than I expected from two of the school's worst grammar pupils."

Then, growing very serious again, she added, "But tell me, do you think 'two', 'eleven' and 'third' are all the same type of numbers? I mean, do you think they express the idea of numbers in exactly the same way?"

"No," said Linda quickly. "I was thinking about that just now. 'Two' and 'eleven' are merely common numbers—one, two, three, four, five, six, seven—aren't they, Madam Adjective? But 'third' is different—"

"Yes," Barry interrupted, " 'third' is different because it expresses the idea of order, of—of rank, you know. Frank White, for instance, didn't come first in our class this year, or second, but third—third 'in *order* of merit' Miss Randal said."

Merely common numbers.

"Quite right, Barry. And because it expresses order, it is called 'ordinal'. And when I am 'third' or 'second' or any other ordinal, humans call me 'ordinal adjective'."

"Oh," cried Linda joyfully, "every, every, everything is so easy in Grammar Kingdom."

"Sir Pronoun told you, I know," the wee lady rapidly continued, "that he often asks questions, and before you go, children, I must tell you that I, too, am often inquisitive."

"And," asked Linda, "are you, also, called 'interrogative' when you are inquisitive?"

"I am. But again I am different from Sir Pronoun in that I don't stand in the place of Miss Noun, but ask a question about her in her very presence—anything I like: 'which?', 'what?'—"

"Oh, how nice!" Barry interrupted. "But I'm afraid you must often give Miss Noun a bad time."

"Not always, though, Barry," Linda corrected, "because when you say 'Which flower?' you can see Madam Adjective there asking her question as 'which?' and Miss Noun standing beside her as 'flower', and yet Madam Adjective is not being a scrap unkind."

Barry was a little upset at that, for he did not want to seem unappreciative, particularly when Madam Adjective had explained herself so kindly. So, to make it better. he said quickly, "I think, madam, you are really a most necessary person. I mean, whatever would sentences do without you? You always seem to have such big, important positions in them."

"Yes, yes, to be sure," the lady agreed, looking pleased. "But I'm not always large or conspicuous by any means. For instance, I don't suppose you've ever realized that I am also those tiny words 'a', 'an' and 'the'."

"Dear me, no," said Linda. "I never knew that before. I thought 'the', 'a' and 'an' were articles."

"So they are," replied the lady, "but 'article' is just the fancy name mortals give me whenever I am 'the', 'a' or 'an'. Do you see?"

Barry and Linda both assured her that they did see. Quite clearly, whereupon she said,

"Well now, as I know how anxious you are to meet the other Parts of Speech, I shan't keep you any longer. Good-bye, children. It's been very pleasant to see you."

"Thank you," said Barry, "and—"

"And we've simply loved meeting you," Linda broke in.

But Sir Desire was slowly though zealously edging away, all agog for their next adventure, and the twins were quick to follow him.

"Good-bye, Madam Adjective! Good-bye!" the three called out together as they moved towards the entrance of the bower.

CHAPTER VI

A TERRIBLE HAPPENING

JUST as they were about to reopen the gate that led into the garden of the Parts of Speech the two children and Sir Desire were startled by a tremendous noise. It seemed as if hundreds of voices were all shouting at once, and as if thousands of footsteps were rushing about hither and thither in absolute confusion.

"Dear me!" exclaimed the little man. "Whatever is happening? Something, to be sure, has gone wrong. Come, let's find out what it is."

And, springing into the garden with Linda and Barry at his heels, he was nearly knocked right over by panic-stricken swarms of Grammar people, all of them shouting at the tops of their voices. Little Miss Noun ran past looking quite terrified. Master Verb was holding her hand and taking the longest strides imaginable, and he, also, was looking greatly alarmed. Even Wee Baby Conjunction was toddling away as fast as her tiny legs could carry her.

But there were not only Parts of Speech, for the crowd was far too large to be composed of them alone. Amongst them, all higgledy-piggledy, were Old Man Full-stop and Tall Boy Semi-colon. Taking the tiniest and quickest of steps was little Lady Comma, followed by a very surprised-looking Mr Exclamation Mark. Sir Capital Letter was one of the most dignified, though he, too, was hurrying for all he was worth. Miss Question

Mark appeared rather shy, but she could run as fast as any of them; and as for Paragraph Esquire, he simply took one long stride to get to the extreme other end of the garden, where he hid behind a large tree.

"Oh Barry, have you hurt yourself?" cried Linda as she happened to look down at the ground and see her brother sprawling there in a most undignified position.

"N-no," he replied, struggling up at last. "It was just Sir Pronoun. No doubt about it, he's awfully rough. Of course, he didn't do it purposely—though it's not the first time he's knocked me over, eh, Lin?" he added with a chuckle. "But—but all the same, I *would* like to know if Grammar Kingdom is coming to an end. It must be a volcano or something."

Their little guide, however, was not looking worried any longer. "Don't be frightened, children," he shouted, as he had to if he wanted to be heard. "It's nothing to worry about. It isn't a volcano—only a kind of landslide."

"Landslide!" Linda repeated. "Why, I should think that was very much something to worry about."

"No, no," Sir Desire replied. "It isn't nearly as bad as you might imagine."

By this time, the confusion was over, for each of the Grammar people had found a good hiding-place, and all that could now be seen of them were their heads peeping out here and there around trees and bushes. And, crowded together at one extreme end of the garden, they were all gazing distrustfully at something at the other end, which the children, looking, found to be one solitary little boy with a sore, bruised head and a sour expression and, waddling to and fro beside him in a lost sort of manner, a foolish-looking goose.

Sir Desire burst into a peal of laughter which rang through

the entire garden. "You see, children," he explained, "there's a silly young man, indeed, who has done exactly what I told you not to do—fallen down head first. Evidently that dark passage was a bit too much for him, and when one of the stones rolled he rolled with it."

"Why," said Barry, almost too surprised to believe himself, "it's Phil Roberts—the only boy in the school worse at grammar than I am. I say, Phil," he called out to him, laughing in spite of himself, "where does it hurt most?"

But Phil took no notice whatsoever. He merely sat on there, scowling away to himself for all he was worth.

Linda was quite worried about him. "But," she said, "couldn't his Desire have told him to be careful, the way you told us?"

At this, the little man burst into another peal of laughter, and then into another and another, after which he pointed to the goose, still waddling stupidly backwards and forwards, and answered, *"His* Desire! Look at it! Could you expect to find any reason in a goose, my dear? Most likely it, also, has a bruise on its head."

And now, not even tender-hearted Linda could restrain a tiny gurgle of amusement.

"You see," continued the little man, "Phil's desire to learn couldn't have been a real and pure one. For instance, hasn't he always been jealous of the boys at school who did better than he did?"

"Yes," said Barry, "I believe he has been."

"Well then, you can see quite easily that he didn't want to learn about the Parts of Speech and their companions because he was interested in them or loved knowledge, but only so that he could beat his school-fellows and scoop in all the praise to himself without letting any one else share a bit of it. To be sure, a very foolish desire! A positive goose!"

Phil now sprang up and began to stamp his feet on the grass in downright bad-temper. More and more angry he grew, and the harder he stamped the more certain did Barry and Linda feel that they could see a big black cloud slowly but surely approaching him and looking as if it meant to swallow him right up. Nearer and nearer it came. Barry and Linda watching it tensely, until at last it arrived, and settled down all round him in the form of thousands of tiny hobgoblins all dressed in black.

"Oh," Linda gasped, "that—that's terrible! They're going to hurt him. Oh please, Sir Desire, what—what can we do?"

But the little man only smiled calmly and said, "You couldn't do anything to help him, Lin, no matter how hard you tried, for those ugly wee imps are all his own ugly

Tiny hobgoblins all dressed in black.

thoughts, and now that he's brought them to life they wouldn't leave him alone for all the world until they've quite finished with him. If you'll notice, my dear, they're divided into several companies. The one on this side is the company of Bad-temper. The one on the other side is that of Jealousy. The one in front of him is that of Hatred, and—"

But before he could say any more, the whole enormous troop had gathered together and, having lifted Phil high into the air, were carrying him away from Grammar Kingdom with all possible speed, much to the relief of the Parts of Speech and their many friends. And the ridiculous goose, having hurried about desperately for a moment or so, simply disappeared into air.

"I hope he'll be at school to-morrow," said Barry, laughing, as he watched the tiny speck in the sky which was all that could now be seen of Phil and his hobgoblins.

"Yes, yes, I hope so," Sir Desire merrily agreed, "although—Well, those imps might carry him anywhere."

CHAPTER VII

MASTER VERB

IT was no time now before all the Parts of Speech and their friends crept out from their hiding-places with a great sigh of relief and, after talking amongst themselves for a few minutes about what they felt to have been their very serious peril and narrow escape, slowly walked off to go on with their usual affairs. Not every single one of them, however, for in a far corner of that lovely garden Master Verb was still to be seen, moving about rather dazedly.

Master Verb, moving about rather dazedly.

Slowly, rather shyly, the children followed their manly little Sir Desire as he went striding up to Master Verb with long, bold steps. But neither of them nor of Sir Desire did Master Verb take any notice whatever.

"He doesn't seem very happy," Linda observed. in a hushed voice. "I suppose Phil and his imps frightened him an extra special lot."

"Oh, he'll soon get over it," the tiny man replied. "He's not miserable really. He's only feeling uncommonly passive—"

"Not at all!" he ejaculated, turning round abruptly and looking even taller and thinner than Sir Pronoun, and a great deal more worn. "You speak most unfairly about me, and so do humans."

"But," Barry objected, "aren't you ever passive, sir? I had an idea that you were, quite often."

"No, no, no," cried Master Verb, very upset. "Although," he added quietly, "no matter how many complaints I put in, none of them ever does anything towards removing the charge of passiveness from me, so I shan't try any more."

"Well then," said Linda, "please tell us, Master Verb, how it happens that you're always thought of as being either passive or active. You must have done *something* to make so many people think like that about you."

"Ah," he sighed, "it's a long sad story. But if you really want to know it, I'll make it as short as possible for you."

"Of course we want to know it," Barry assured him.

"Well, to begin with, although I'm the one always said to be either passive or active, in reality I'm nothing of the kind. My subject is."

"What do you mean by your subject?" Barry asked. "You're not a king, are you, Master Verb?"

"Dear, dear, dear," replied the tall gentleman, "nothing like that. Although, in spite of all that's said about me, I am, I must admit, rather an important person in Grammar Kingdom. But let me see, now, where were we? Oh yes, we were talking about my subject. Well, sometimes my subject is Miss Noun, sometimes Sir Pronoun, sometimes a short phrase."

The children looked a bit puzzled, and Master Verb laughed, for he rather enjoyed puzzling people. But, as had the other folk in Grammar Land, Master Verb had formed quite a liking for the twins since their arrival there, and had promised his better self to make things as easy as possible for them, so—

"You see," he continued, "I am the Part of Speech who, in

one way or another, expresses action; and when I appear in a sentence (expressing that action) the person or thing carrying out the action is known as my 'subject'. Now do you understand?"

"I think so," Linda replied, "but—but I can't be quite sure."

"I see. Well, I'll just bring along a sentence for you. That'll fix it up."

Linda glanced across at Barry. "Bring along a sentence!" she murmured. "That does sound funny."

But Barry had not time to suggest anything before there came swinging across, hanging in a row from a long cobweb, the words:

THE DOOR SHUT

And not only this, but there came running along hand in hand at the same moment Madam Adjective and Miss Noun. Madam Adjective took her place below THE. Her little companion stood below DOOR, and Master Verb then walked up and stood on the other side of Miss Noun below SHUT.

"Oh, how lovely!" cried Linda. "Look, there is Madam Adjective being an article, and Miss Noun is 'door', and Master Verb is 'shut'."

"Yes, yes," Barry brought in eagerly. "And he's expressing action, too, just as he said he did, because if the door shut it was acting in some way, wasn't it?"

"Exactly," called out Master Verb. "And now you've said all by yourself what my subject is in this sentence, which was what I wanted to show you."

"Yes," said Linda, "it's Miss Noun as 'door', because 'door' is carrying out the action 'shut', and so *must* be your subject. Isn't that what you said a moment ago, Master Verb?"

"Indeed it is. And now that you know what I mean by my

"She looks quite lively and alert."

subject, I'll see what I can do about straightening up this active and passive business."

"Oh yes, I'd forgotten all about that," Barry confessed.

"Well," Master Verb continued, "before I change this sentence in front of you, I want you to look carefully at Miss Noun. She looks quite lively and alert, doesn't she? That's because she's acting—quite plainly so. Yet when this is the case, I'm the one who's called 'active'. Now, do any of you think that's fair, or even reasonable?"

"She looks absolutely passive."

The twins looked at one another inquiringly, but Master Verb hurried on without waiting for an answer. "Now, now," he said, "keep on watching our sentence carefully, you two!"

Quickly Linda and Barry fastened their eyes on the swinging sentence again, and did not as much as blink, even though they saw the word SHUT sliding along the cobweb as if by magic, to make room for WAS which now appeared from nowhere and settled itself between SHUT and DOOR. And at the same time they noticed a dreamy expression stealing into Miss Noun's eyes, until it seemed as if she was merely standing up in her sleep. So the sentence now read:

THE DOOR WAS SHUT

and Master Verb took his place below both WAS and SHUT.

Linda and Barry gazed at it for some time before Master Verb spoke.

"It doesn't seem to me," he said at last, "that there's anything active about Miss Noun any longer. In fact, she looks absolutely passive, because she, as 'door', is not doing a thing for herself. Somebody has come along and shut her without a scrap of her help. Yet to whom, in this case, should the description 'passive' be attached but to me! Now, what do you think of that?"

"Awful," said Barry, with deep feeling.

"Yes, quite!" Linda agreed. "But what I'm thinking about most just now is how lovely and easy you are to understand after all, Master Verb."

"Hm, quite nice!" replied the tall gentleman. "But I haven't told you half the things about me yet."

"No," said Barry with a laugh, "I don't think you have. You've always seemed to me as full of mysteries as a crossword puzzle."

At that, Master Verb chuckled with great delight. "Sometimes," he said suddenly, "when I'm feeling lenient I let things off lightly, but other times, when I'm not as lenient, I get quite a number of things concerned with me."

"Goodness!" Linda exclaimed. "That does sound like a riddle, Master Verb. And—and is it so very unpleasant, then, to be concerned with you?"

"That all depends," said Master Verb, looking solemn. "For

instance, in the sentence 'John broke the vase' you can see me as 'broke'—the action. And the one carrying out the action is—"

"Is 'John'," said Barry.

"So 'John' is your subject, Master Verb," Linda added quickly.

"Yes, yes. Well, John may be feeling quite all right about it, but then, you see, he's not the only one concerned with me—with the breaking, that is. The vase is also concerned and is, I'm afraid, feeling the very opposite of quite all right."

The two children laughed merrily, then Barry began to look puzzled. "But Master Verb, if you call 'John' your 'subject', what would you call 'vase'?"

" 'Vase' is my 'object'," the gentleman replied. "It is the thing acted *upon*."

"And must your object always be Miss Noun, or could it, also, be Sir Pronoun or a short phrase?" asked Barry.

"It could be, as you say, Sir Pronoun or a short phrase," said Master Verb, "and very often is, too."

"But," said Linda. "you don't have to act upon something always, do you, Master Verb? In the sentence 'The door shut' or 'The girl walked' you have no object, have you?"

"Quite right, Linda. Often I have no object, and then I'm called an 'intransitive' verb."

"Why?" asked Barry.

"I suppose because, when I do have an object, I'm called a 'transitive' verb," he answered promptly.

"That seems a fairly good reason," said Linda.

"And now, there is something else puzzling me about you," Barry announced.

"Surely not!" said Master Verb.

"Well," Barry continued, "Sir Pronoun talked to us a lot

about being first, second and third person, and yet I seem to remember person and *you* being mentioned together. Is that right, or am I only dreaming?"

"It's very much right, and quite easy to explain," Master Verb replied. "To begin with, you have already seen how Madam Adjective shares her inquisitive and 'pointing out' qualities with Sir Pronoun; and you must know that I too share some of my qualities with other Parts of Speech."

"And personhood is one," said Linda.

"Right. You have often heard it said that a verb agrees with its subject in person and number, haven't you?"

"Yes," said Barry, "but—"

"No, there are no buts about it. It's all very simple. I'm sure you would never say 'I talks' or 'he talk', would you?"

"Why, of course not," said Linda, thinking what a silly question that was to ask.

"You can see, then, that I have to alter my form according to my subject, can't you? In other words, I have to 'agree' with my subject. And my goodness, if I disagreed, there'd be an upheaval of the first order in Grammar Kingdom. Why, even King Speech would believe himself personally insulted, and as for me—well, I'd be lucky if I escaped a charge of downright treason, I can tell you."

"Dear me, how terrible!" Linda exclaimed.

"So," Master Verb continued, now in a calmer tone, "when you say 'he talks', 'he' is my subject and also third person, which means that I have to be third person too."

At this Linda looked rather thoughtful. "What a lot of copying you have to do, Master Verb," she remarked. "It seems a bit like follow-the-leader, doesn't it, Barry?"

"Yes, Lin, but it's hardly polite to say so," Barry answered softly. Then, more loudly, he asked, "And what about number, Master Verb?"

"Number," the tall gentleman replied, "is just as simple, for when you say 'he', 'she', or 'it', you mean one thing or person only—a *single* one—don't you?"

"Yes."

"Well, then you call the number 'singular'. But when you say 'we' or 'they', you are speaking about more than one person or thing, aren't you?"

"Yes."

"And when you are speaking of more than one, the number is called 'plural'. That's all there is to know about number."

"I see," said Barry. "And you have to agree with your subject in number. Yet it is just as right to say 'I walk' as it is to say 'we walk'. You don't seem to put yourself out very much to agree with the different kinds of number there, Master Verb."

Suddenly the tall gentleman gripped his head in his hands and took a few strides up and down in a most worried manner. Then he stopped again in front of Barry and looked—strangely enough for a big fellow like that—as if he might any moment burst into tears.

"Dear, dear, dear!" he exclaimed. "I'm always being reminded of that. Yet it's just my way of agreeing—just my way. Can't anybody understand? Honestly, I spend a full three-quarters of my life in the Grammar Court, on the never-ending charge of 'irregularity'. Goodness knows what will happen to me in the end."

"Oh," said Linda, "what a nuisance! But can't you do anything about it, Master Verb? I mean, couldn't you try to be a little more law-abiding?"

"I *have* tried, often and often," he answered, "but it always takes me so long to get used to changes that I simply slip back to the old ways again time after time. And now, right inside me, I'm afraid—yes. I'm very much afraid—that I've pretty well given myself up as impossible."

"So have many people," said Barry, with a boyish grin.

"Another trouble is," continued Master Verb, "that when I do try to change myself for each different person, as in 'I am, you are, he is'—even then, and for that very reason, mind you—there's still such an outcry against me that I haven't the courage to alter myself again when I come to the plural number and so, having chosen the 'are', I remain that for 'we', 'you' plural and 'they'."

"An outcry by whom?" asked Linda.

"By one section of the jury that has grown so used to my not changing to agree that it now looks upon any change at all as an irregularity. You see," he whined pitifully, "everything I do is sure to be irregular as far as someone or other is concerned."

Meanwhile Barry had been thinking hard, and had realized that in all the cases he could think of except the verb 'to be', his tall friend was equally thoughtless of both person and number, paying his respects only to third person singular, and then merely by picking up a stray S from somewhere in the most careless fashion. But, seeing that the cloud of misery on Master Verb's face was only just now beginning to lift, he could not bring himself to say anything about this shameful discovery.

"So far," continued Master Verb, "I've only spoken to you about me when I'm 'present tense'—when I'm acting at the *present* time. But you must know that I have a very good memory, as well as being something of a prophet. When I recall past actions I am said to be in the 'past tense', and when I prophesy what is to happen in the future I am said to be in the 'future tense'."

The Little Grammar People

"And do you change yourself for past and future a little more than you do for person and number?" Barry could not help asking.

Whereupon the tall gentleman again looked very alarmed. "Ss-sh!" he exclaimed, glancing here, there and everywhere in a dozen or more different places at once. "Please, I beg of you, don't remind the jury!"

"Why?" asked Linda, her eyes shining with amusement, even though she tried hard to keep them serious and worried-looking.

"Because every time my past and future are mentioned too loudly, that section of the jury which does happen to be in favour of change gets itself very much up in arms and threatens me with all sorts of things."

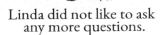

Linda did not like to ask any more questions.

So of course, Linda did not like to ask any more questions, but she thought for herself as quickly as she could. Lots and lots of verbs hurried through her mind in their past and future tenses, and she saw that none of them except "to be" altered in any way. First of all the past:

I walked   we walked
you walked   you (plural) walked
he walked   they walked

then the future:

I shall walk   we shall walk
you will walk   you (plural) will walk
he will walk   they will walk

Master Verb

Of course, there were, in the future, the changes of "will" and "shall"; but after all, those were only parts of "to be". A grave situation!

Master Verb, gazing at the twins intently, felt so afraid of what they might next say about his irregularities that at last he could stand it no longer, and called out, "Well, children, there's absolutely nothing more to say. I'm very pleased to have met you, but now you—you might oblige me by going."

Barry and Linda were so amused at his uneasiness that they merely stood where they were and laughed at him.

"Go! Go!" he repeated urgently.

"He's in his 'imperative mood' now," said Sir Desire. "He's giving an order, and won't stand any nonsense. We'd better run."

So he and the twins ran to the other end of the garden as fast as their legs would carry them, and when they looked back again they could see no more of Master Verb, and wondered if he had been summoned to another trial in the Grammar Court.

CHAPTER VIII

LADY ADVERB

"DO you think we could possibly find the Grammar Court, Sir Desire?" asked Barry. " 'Cause I'm sure that's where Master Verb has disappeared to, and I'd simply love to hear what's being said about him."

"Yes, I think we could go," he replied. "How do you feel about it, Lin?"

"Oh, every bit the same as Barry," said Linda. "I've heard so much about courts and juries, you know, yet I've never met them in person. It would be great fun."

"Come along, then," said the little man, and once more he led the way out of the huge garden. But this time he did not go towards the bower of Madam Adjective. Instead, he chose a long cobble-stone path which seemed to have no end to it. On and on he walked, followed always by the two children, who had so much to think about in connection with their many Grammar Kingdom adventures that neither of them even dreamed of growing tired.

After quite a long time, however, Sir Desire said, "It's an awful shame we can't travel as quickly as the Parts of Speech, isn't it? They seem to fly here, there and everywhere as quickly as thought itself. Remarkable creatures. Never mind, though, we're nearly there now."

And just as he said this, the twins were amazed to hear a loud chorus of shouting.

Lady Adverb

"Something is being approved of, all right," Linda remarked.

"Or perhaps disapproved of," suggested Sir Desire.

There were no stone or brick walls to the Grammar Court. It was simply a little grassy area surrounded by a rickety wooden fence, and crowded along the edges with tiny people. On one side was the jury, consisting of every imaginable Grammar person. And, to be sure, on the other side, all alone, was Master Verb, looking very downcast. Supervising the whole assembly from a broken tree-stump was the judge, and in the middle of the grassy patch was an extremely stern-looking barrister.

It appeared that this session had been going on for quite a long time and was now drawing near its close, with the jury rapidly becoming unanimous.

"Who is it, ladies and gentlemen, who is constantly insulting our gracious sovereign King Speech?" the stern barrister was saying. "Who is it who is responsible for the endless abuse showered upon the honourable English language by every one who studies Reason and Common Sense? Why, ladies and gentlemen, there is only one answer to my question—Master Verb! Master Verb, with his continual irregularities!"

Here there occurred a sensation in court. Every one seemed very much moved. In fact, all the members of the jury took out their pocket handkerchiefs and made ample use of them, so overcome were they by horror and indignation.

"There you see him," continued the barrister. "There you see this Master Verb, who can respect neither number nor person. An outlaw, ladies and gentlemen—a positive rebel, a villain!"

Again there was a sensation in court, and by this time the jury seemed quite unanimous.

"Consider your foolish positions in sentences."

Lady Adverb

"Oh, poor Master Verb!" Linda exclaimed.

The jury, growing more furious every moment, was now beginning to suggest all kinds of violence, such as throwing Master Verb out of Grammar Kingdom altogether.

But when the judge heard this, he evidently thought it was high time he interfered, for he suddenly jumped up on to his smart little feet and, shouting louder than any of them, commanded:

"Order! Order! Silence in the Court! The members of the jury are, I am certain, in the act of losing their heads. May I call their attention to their own desperate situation if it happened that our valuable citizen Master Verb were banished from the Kingdom? Ladies and gentlemen, I beg of you, consider your foolish positions in sentences were it not for Master Verb!"

And now there occurred another sensation, but this time in favour of the poor abused prisoner, for the people in Grammar Kingdom can change their minds just as quickly and as completely as mortals can.

"You are therefore, Master Verb," the little judge announced, his face beaming with triumph, since he felt that he had proved himself to be a great orator, "you are therefore, according to the law of Grammar Kingdom, declared Not Guilty."

By this time Barry's face was also beaming, and " 'Urrah! 'Urrah! 'Urrah!" he shouted at the top of his voice.

But the judge turned a grave, disapproving glance upon him at that. "Young man," he said. "would you have the goodness to pick up all those H's you've just dropped? They make the Court look so untidy—quite uproarious, in fact."

Following the judge's accusing finger, Barry looked down at the ground, and imagine his surprise at seeing, scattered about over it, three large H's in varying stages of collapse!

Three large H's in varying stages of collapse.

"Oh, I—I'm very sorry, Mr Judge," he exclaimed. "but really, I've so often heard people say—well, that word, the way I said it."

It was an uncomfortable moment, during which every one in the Court was absolutely silent, and all eyes were fixed upon Barry and his clumsy efforts to gather up those awkward, sprawling H's which seemed to be all arms and legs and very little sense. But as soon as the last one had been tucked firmly away, legs and all, in one of Barry's large-sized pockets, everybody's attention was removed from the incident, and Master Verb, in the highest of spirits, prepared to leave the Court.

Lady Adverb

The two children and Sir Desire rushed up to congratulate him, and also a little lady they had not met before. In reply, he doffed his cap, bowed low, beamed all over and, in a far lighter-hearted tone than they had heard him use before, exclaimed, "Let me introduce you, children, to my friend and helper Lady Adverb."

The lady said she was delighted to be introduced, and so did Linda and Barry.

"And now, as my friend is going straight back to where I think you're going—to our garden of sunshine and leisure—I shall leave her in your keeping, children," he said. "I think you should find each other good company. I have many things to attend to, and so must hurry away. Good-bye!"

And immediately the tall gentleman disappeared, leaving his four good friends to face the cobble-stone path once more. It was quite a long while before the twins or their two small companions attempted to speak, but several times Barry, who could not help looking upon Lady Adverb with a good bit of suspicion, took a sly, sidelong glance at her when he was sure she was not noticing, and at last he stammered awkwardly, "Lady Adverb, are you—I mean, do you think you're just as nice as all the other Parts of Speech? That is, you know, do you think that when Lin and I get to know you properly we'll be able to—to like you just as much?"

"Well, I hope so," she answered, laughing. "I always try to be nice, and I certainly hope you'll like me."

"You know," said Linda, "I'm rather surprised to see that you're not the least bit like Madam Adjective to look at, 'cause I've mixed you up with her so much that I was quite sure you were exactly the same all the time, and only pretending to be different."

"Dear me," the little lady exclaimed, "that *is* a serious state

The cobble-stone path once more.

of affairs! But of course, I know that humans do mix us up badly at times. Oh dear, oh dear! And we Grammar people, the same as mortal people, do like to be individual."

"Yes, I suppose you do," Barry agreed. "But now that we see how different you are to look at, would you mind telling us, Lady Adverb, how you are different in—well, in other ways?"

Lady Adverb

Again the little lady laughed. "Now, that's a tall order, Barry," she said. "In other ways! That might mean anything—and everything. So I suppose the sooner we start the better. Well, to begin with, you can tell by my very name that my chief duty is quite different from Madam Adjective's."

"And what is that?" asked Linda.

"Why, to *add* something to Master *Verb*."

Barry looked at her with large, wide-open eyes. "Good gracious!" he exclaimed. "But what sort of something do you add to him, and—and where do you add it? I mean, do you—do you make him taller, or wider, or—"

But Lady Adverb, with a tiny chuckle of merriment, interrupted him. "I add to his meaning, Barry," she explained.

"Oh," said both the twins together, but not very enthusiastically, for they were still a good bit in the dark as to what she meant.

"Oh come, there's really nothing mysterious about me at all," she assured them. "Let me show you. When, for instance, you say 'Mary runs quickly', you have Master Verb there as 'runs', and you have me there as 'quickly'. You see, I explain him, or say something about him, and so I add to his meaning."

Linda took a little hop and skip when she heard that, and cried out excitedly, "But is that all there is to know about you, Lady Adverb? Is that really all?"

"Well, nearly," she replied, "but there are a few other things too, because, although I spend most of my time adding meaning to

Lady Adverb.

59

Master Verb, I devote some of it to myself, and also to Madam Adjective and Small Boy Preposition (whom you will soon be meeting)."

"Gracious, that's funny!" said Barry.

"Oh no it isn't—not really," she answered quickly. "It's perfectly simple. After all, to add meaning to myself, Madam Adjective and Small Boy Preposition is just as easy as it is to add it to Master Verb."

"Yes, maybe it is." Barry agreed after some hesitation.

"But, that being the case, you should have four names instead of one, shouldn't you? Adverb, Adadjective, Adpreposition and Adadverb."

Lady Adverb shook her head and laughed. "Oh dear, no," she said. "Nothing of the kind, Barry. If you had your way, you *would* confuse poor humans. Fancy one Grammar person having four different names! Dear me, dear me! I could never put up with that—and neither could you. And besides, my name is quite fitting since, you remember, it's adding meaning to Master Verb that takes up most of my time."

"I've been thinking, it would be awfully funny adding meaning to oneself," said Linda. "Don't you find that rather hard to do, Lady Adverb?"

"Not at all, Linda, because what you've been used to all your life is easy for you."

"And you've always been used to that?"

"Yes. I'll show you how. Let us think of our old friend 'Mary runs quickly'."

"Our old sentence, you mean," said Barry, with a grin.

"Oh, but friend too," Lady Adverb insisted.

"Yes, of course friend," Linda brought in quickly. "Everything and every one in Grammar Kingdom is a friend to us now."

60

Lady Adverb

"Oh, all right," said Barry. still grinning. "Let's think of our old sentence friend, then—'Mary runs quickly'. 'Mary' is Miss Noun being proper, 'runs' is Master Verb being present, and 'quickly' is you being-well, adding meaning to Master Verb."

"Right. And now, if you said 'Mary runs very quickly', what Part of Speech do you think 'very' would be?"

The twins thought for a long while, but neither of them seemed to be thinking in the right direction, for they could not find any answer at all, and finally it was Lady Adverb herself who had to find one for them.

"You said just now, Barry, that 'quickly' was myself—an adverb. And if you think a minute, you'll see that 'very' is adding something to 'quickly'. It isn't letting it be just quickly; it's making it be *very* quickly. And so, as it is adding something to it, isn't it myself adding to myself?"

"Oh yes, of course it is," cried the two children together. "And," Barry continued, "the same thing would happen in the sentence 'John wrote too carelessly', wouldn't it? You are there as 'carelessly', adding meaning to Master Verb who is 'wrote'. And there you are again as 'too', adding meaning to yourself this time—to yourself as 'carelessly'."

"Quite right," she replied. "So you see, I'm not nearly as hard to understand as you've always thought, am I?"

"No, no," said Linda.

"And now," the little lady continued eagerly, "if you said 'This roadway is rather long', what Part of Speech would 'long' be?"

"Madam Adjective," said Barry, "as it is describing 'roadway'."

"Right. And you can see that 'rather' is adding a certain meaning to 'long'. The roadway is not just long, or very long. It is *rather* long."

The Little Grammar People

"Yes, yes, of course we can see," said Linda. " 'Rather' is you, Lady Adverb, and it is you adding meaning to Madam Adjective. Oh, this is all lovely. And—and what happens when you add something to Small Boy Preposition?"

"Well, you haven't met him yet, so that's a bit harder to explain. But you'll just have to take my word for it that in the sentence 'We are quite near the garden now', 'near' is Small Boy Preposition."

"Oh," cried Linda, "Well, in that case, 'quite' must be you, Lady Adverb, as that, certainly, is adding meaning to 'near'."

When the little lady said that sentence, the four travellers really were near the garden, and just as Linda was finishing her explanation they pushed aside a few large bushes and went into it.

"And could you explain to us now," asked Barry, "that funny expression 'adverb of time'? Can you really be 'of time'?

And if so, what on earth does it mean, and what does it feel like, and how do you manage it?"

"Good gracious!" Lady Adverb exclaimed, bursting into a ripple of merriment that sounded exactly like a field of magic bluebells all ringing together at midnight. "What a lot of questions all at once!"

"Yes," said Barry, "but what I mean is that I thought you spent all your time adding something to Parts of Speech. But that expression sounds as if you must also add something to time. Yet time isn't a Part of Speech any more than I am, and—and so, you see, it's altogether very puzzling."

"No, no, it isn't!" The little lady seemed very decided on that point. "I can play about and amuse myself with the idea of time—and with the idea of place too, by the way—just as easily as I can with Master Verb, Madam Adjective, Small Boy Preposition and myself. 'I like to walk where the buttercups grow.' That's a sentence in which the idea of place is expressed, isn't it?"

"Yes."

"And tell me, now, what is the actual word in it that manages to express that idea?"

"I think," said Linda, "that it must be 'where'."

"Quite right," said Lady Adverb. "So that—"

"Yes, yes," Barry interrupted excitedly. "So that 'where' is you, isn't it?"

"It is indeed, Barry. And of course, humans would call 'where' an 'adverb of place'. And it's the same kind of thing exactly that happens with time. If your friend said to you, 'At what time will you be at the station?' and you replied, 'I shall be there when the clock strikes three', you would be using me as 'when', wouldn't you? And humans would say that you were using an 'adverb of time'."

"Oh, I see," said Linda. "Yes, Lady Adverb, you were right. It isn't a scrap puzzling after all. But—but there's still another question I'd like to ask you. How is it that all this time we've been silly enough to think you were exactly the same as Madam Adjective?"

Lady Adverb gave careful thought to the matter for a second or two before replying that "Most likely it was because there are some words, like 'fast' for instance, which are sometimes Madam Adjective and sometimes myself, without changing their appearance in the least. But if," she added, "whenever you meet one of them in a sentence, you examine it carefully and see exactly what it's doing, I'm sure you'll never mix me up with Madam Adjective again. Let me show you what I mean. You may speak about a 'fast horse', or you may say that the horse 'runs fast'. 'Fast' looks and sounds the same in both cases, doesn't it? And yet in one it is Madam Adjective, and in the other it is Lady Adverb."

"Yes, that right, isn't it, Barry?" said Linda, giving her brother's sleeve a little tug, "because in the first case 'fast' is describing Miss Noun—Miss Noun as 'horse'—and so it must be Madam Adjective."

"And in the second case," said Barry, " 'fast' is adding meaning to Master Verb, as 'runs', and so it must be Lady Adverb."

Their eyes were filled with delight to the very brim as they both turned toward Lady Adverb again to thank her for having made herself so easy to understand, but, to their disappointment, she was there no longer. As seemed to be quite a habit amongst all these shy little Parts of Speech, she had suddenly and completely disappeared.

CHAPTER IX

SMALL BOY PREPOSITION

"I WONDER where she could have gone to," said Barry.

"I wonder where all of them could have gone to," said Linda.

"Most likely," said Sir Desire, "they've all gone to crowd themselves into some poor sentence, quite regardless of whether it's got room for them or not."

But at that moment a friendly, boyish voice sounded right behind them. "Hullo!" it said.

And, looking round, the twins saw standing in front of them another Part of Speech.

"Hullo!" Linda answered. And, remembering something Lady Adverb had said, she added, "Are you, by any chance, Small Boy Preposition?"

"I am," he replied. "I see you've already heard about me. Yes, I was just on my way to make an adverbial phrase when Lady Adverb herself came along and told me you were waiting to meet me. She very kindly offered to go in my place, so here I am."

"Oh, is that allowed?" asked Barry, much surprised.

"Of course it's allowed," replied the little boy. "It is, after all, Lady Adverb's place, and it's only when she's busy somewhere else that I go along instead. But I always regard myself as the second best thing, you understand."

"No, I'm afraid I don't understand," said Linda.

The Little Grammar People

The little boy smiled broadly. "Well," he said, "I'll soon show you what I mean. In the sentence 'He spoke angrily', 'spoke' is Master Verb, isn't it?"

"Yes."

"And what is 'angrily'?"

"Why, Lady Adverb, because it's adding meaning to 'spoke'," said Barry.

"Right. But now, suppose Lady Adverb didn't feel like going into that sentence, what do you think she would do? She *could* do something, you know."

"I can't guess at all," said Barry, after a short pause. "Well, she'd simply ask me if I could help her, and I'd promise her to do my best. Then I'd call Miss Noun, and we'd hurry along to the sentence together. So that the sentence now, instead of being 'He spoke angrily', would be 'He spoke with anger'."

"Oh," said Linda.

"You see, I am there as 'with', and Miss Noun is there beside me as 'anger'."

"And Miss Noun is in her abstract or untouchable mood, isn't she?" asked Barry.

"She is," the small boy replied.

"Well," said Linda, "what a very good way out!"

"That," the little lad answered, "is what I'm not so sure about, for you see, although the sentence means the same thing as it would have if Lady Adverb had been there instead of us, it's ever so much clumsier."

"Yes, it is rather clumsy,"

"Then I'd call Miss Noun."

66

Barry agreed. "But still, it's the best you can do, and—well, it's sporting of you to do anything at all, really."

At which the little preposition boy grew quite half an inch taller with pride. But Linda soon had another question for him to answer.

"And do you help only Lady Adverb, or some of the other Parts of Speech as well?" she asked him.

"Not only Lady Adverb by any means," he said. And, thrusting his hands into his trouser pockets, looked very important indeed. "Often and often Madam Adjective sends me a message by butterfly post that reads something like this: 'Preposition, my pet, I've just been called upon to be present in a sentence, but it's so cool and comfortable here in my bower that I feel awfully lazy about it. And besides, your legs are younger than mine. So be a dear and help me out of it.' "

"And do you help her out?" asked Linda.

"Of course I do. What do you s'pose would be the use of me in Grammar Kingdom if I didn't?"

"And does Miss Noun go along with you too—the same as she does when you're helping Lady Adverb?"

"Yes, but she isn't always in her abstract mood. First of all, though, suppose you had the phrase 'a beautiful song'. 'Beautiful' would be Madam Adjective, wouldn't it?"

"Yes."

"But when I go to take her place, the phrase becomes 'a song of beauty'."

"Yes, yes," cried Linda. "There is

"A message by butterfly post."

67

Miss Noun as 'beauty', being abstract. And this time you are 'of'."

"Quite right, Lin. But I told you just now that Miss Noun isn't abstract always—and when she isn't, things get mighty awkward."

"How is that?" asked Barry.

"If you think of the phrase 'a blue-eyed girl', I'll tell you."

"We're thinking," said Linda.

"Well, what Part of Speech do you think 'blue-eyed' would be?"

"Madam Adjective, of course," said Barry.

"Yes. Now Madam Adjective, for some reason or other, mightn't feel like putting in an appearance, and then, of course, I'd go along with Miss Noun and do my best; but I couldn't do very much because, after all, Madam Adjective herself simply can't be done without in that phrase. Can you see why?"

"Oh, I know," cried Linda. "Don't tell me. She can't be done without because the phrase, with your help, would have to be 'a girl with blue eyes', wouldn't it?"

"Yes."

"So that 'blue' would have to be in it still, and 'blue' is Madam Adjective."

"Right. So you see, she has to come along, in spite of everything."

The twins laughed heartily.

"Serves her jolly well right for being so lazy," said Barry.

And Small Boy Preposition laughed too, for he could always enjoy a joke against his friends Annette Adverb and Arabella Adjective. "So now you can understand," he continued at last, "what I meant when I told you that I was on my way to make an adverbial phrase, can't you?"

"Yes, of course, quite easily," said Barry. "You were going

along with Miss Noun to take the place of Lady Adverb. And if you'd been going to take Madam Adjective's place, I dare say you'd have been called a—an 'adjectival phrase'. Is that right?"

"Quite," agreed the small boy delightedly. "And you've always been so puzzled by adverbial and adjectival phrases!"

"Yes, we have indeed. But how do you know about that?" asked Linda.

"How do you think I could help knowing?" he replied, grinning mischievously.

"But," said Barry thoughtfully, "you're not always 'of' and 'with', are you?"

"Good heavens no," he answered, looking very important again. "And I'm not always kept busy with adverbial and adjectival phrases, either. For instance, in the sentence 'She was standing against the wall', I, of course, am 'against'; but you can see that I'm not taking either Madam Adjective's place or Lady Adverb's. In fact, I'm taking nobody's place but my own. I've gone there entirely on my own account and everything."

"Yes, but I'm afraid you're being a wee bit boastful about it," said Linda softly.

"Course I'm not!" he objected hotly, and looked so injured that Barry thought it was high time to change the subject, and tumbled himself into the conversation with, "At—at school we've been told that you 'govern' certain words, old chap. Does that mean that you rule them—you know, reign over them?

"N-no, not quite," the little lad replied, as if he would very much have liked to be able to say yes. "That simply means that I come before them. You see, my name, Preposition, has been made up out of two Latin words—one that means 'placed' and the other 'before'."

"Oh, I say, that's two more words Latin has lent us!" cried Barry, seeming highly impressed by the fact.

But Linda was still thinking of the governing, so she said, "Well, in the sentence 'I went with her', 'with' is you, and 'her' is Sir Pronoun."

"Yes."

"Then, as 'with' comes before 'her', it would be said to govern 'her'?"

"Yes," said the small boy, "naturally it would."

"And," Barry added, "in the sentence 'She was near home', 'near' is you and comes before 'home', which is Miss Noun, so that 'near' governs 'home'. Is that right?"

"Quite right."

"Oh," Linda cried out suddenly, "but how jolly grammar is, isn't it, Barry? Isn't it, Sir Desire? Every little teeny bit of it!"

And then Small Boy Preposition's eyes sparkled as brightly as her own. "Well," he said cheerily, tilting his head up into the air and pushing his hands down deeper into his pockets, "now I'm off. And that means that you've only got one more Part of Speech to meet—Wee Baby Conjunction. She's ever so small, and she does an awful lot of baby talk, but she's a nice little thing. You'll like her, I think."

And so, after saying good-bye to the Preposition boy and wishing him well, the two children and Sir Desire stood straining their eyes in every direction, wondering where the last and tiniest Part of Speech would come from.

CHAPTER X

INTERJECTION ESQUIRE

"LAST and tiniest Part of Speech indeed!" said a sharp, indignant little voice near by.

The children and Sir Desire looked everywhere, but there was nothing to be seen.

"Yes, yes," the same voice went on, "you can't even see me, and yet Wee Baby Conjunction is called the tiniest Part of Speech—and the last! I suppose I'm too small to be recognized even."

And just then, as if by chance, Barry happened to notice, amongst the tall grasses and hollyhocks right beside him, a little being no larger than a fair-sized frog. But it was not a frog; it was an elf, dressed all in a beautiful moss-like green, and stretching his head up as far as he could, trying to see the tops of the two children.

Immediately, with a cry of delight. Barry stooped down and rested his hand, palm upward on the

It was an elf.

ground beside the tiny creature. And the elf, understanding what was expected of him, turned a sudden somersault and landed neatly in the very middle of that enormous hand. Barry then lifted him ever so gently, scarcely breathing lest his hand should jerk or tremble.

"Look, look, Lin!" he said, trying to speak softly, and his voice husky with excitement. "What do you think of him? I say, don't you wish we could take him home with us?"

"My, oh my!" Linda replied. And that seemed to be just about all she could manage to say for a moment. Then, whispering rather timidly and not moving even so much as to blink, she added. "I wonder who on earth he can be, Barry?"

But long before Barry could make any suggestion, the elf stretched himself up to his full height, and answered in a high, shrill voice, "My name is Interjection Esquire."

"Yes, of course," said Linda. "I'd forgotten. You'd have to be Interjection. as that's the only other Part of Speech there is except Wee Baby Conjunction. Yet you'd gone right out of my mind, I'm afraid."

At this, the elf pouted sourly. "I seem to go right out of everybody's mind," he remarked, "though I can't imagine what the world would do without me."

"No, neither can I," said Linda. But she only said that to be polite, for in reality she had no idea as to why he should be so important.

"Whatever would humans do if they couldn't say 'Hullo!' and 'Good-bye!' to one another, and if they couldn't shout 'Hurrah!' and 'Bravo!' when they were pleased about something?" the elf continued, still looking much aggrieved.

"I really don't know," said Barry, "but I think they'd sure to be fairly miserable."

"Quite, quite!" agreed the elf, jumping up and down several

times in a most imperative manner. "Why, they wouldn't be humans at all if they couldn't be the whole time protesting and exclaiming about something."

"Exclaiming?" Linda repeated questioningly.

"Yes. Or in other words, using me and then Mr Exclamation Mark straight after me."

"And does that give them so much pleasure?" she asked, still rather bewildered.

"Indeed it does," he replied, "and with reason, too, because that's such a short and easy way of saying what they want to. Just suppose you were at a concert, and liked one of the singers so much that you wanted to hear her sing again."

"Yes," said Barry, "we're supposing."

"Well, don't you think it would be perfectly shocking and tiring and impossible to have to shout, above all the noise of clapping, 'Thank you. That was beautifully sung. Please sing for us again', or something of that sort?"

"My word yes," said Barry.

"Well," the little fellow announced, standing up very straight and tall, smoothing down his moss-coloured coat and flicking the long end of his cap back over his shoulder, "all this difficulty is done away with by none other than me!"

But Linda looked somewhat doubtful. "You'd have to be as clever as clever could be if that were true," she said.

"That's just it," he replied proudly. "The fact is that I *am* as clever as clever can be, for, instead of having to say all those words at your concert, you'd only have to say 'Encore!' That is, you'd only have to use me. Oh," he added after a pause,

"I am as clever as clever can be."

"and of course, that funny-looking little thing after me would be Mr Exclamation Mark."

"Well, well," said Barry. "And you know, I've never thought of it quite like that before. You and Mr Exclamation Mark are certainly well worth remembering, Interjection Esquire."

"Oh yes." Linda brought in eagerly. "And I'm sure Barry and I, at least, will never forget you again, will we, Barry?"

Whereupon the tiny elf appeared thoroughly pleased and amused, for he gurgled, chuckled and laughed so heartily that at last there seemed to be no elf about him at all, but only the most curious mixture imaginable of gurgle, chuckle and laugh. And, funniest thing of all, this mixture, after hovering about for a moment somewhere—it was awfully hard to guess exactly where—suddenly finished on the top of a swaying stalk of bell flowers with something like an exclamation mark.

Interjection Esquire had disappeared.

CHAPTER XI

WEE BABY CONJUNCTION

THE children and Sir Desire had not long been wondering where the last Part of Speech would come from and what she would look like when Linda pointed suddenly to an enormous mushroom and burst into a peal of joyous laughter. It was far larger than any mushroom she or Barry had ever seen, and underneath it, clinging to its stalk, was a wee baby girl with wide-open eyes and a startled expression.

"Oh, what a darling!" Linda exclaimed. "She's the one I'd like to take home most of all, Barry."

And with this she quickly ran right across to the giant mushroom, longing to gather the little baby thing up in her arms and cuddle her, but not quite liking to take such a liberty, especially as she seemed shyer than all the other Parts of Speech put together, and continued looking startled even after Barry and Sir Desire had joined Linda and spoken many coaxing, friendly words to her.

"And so you're what they call Wee Baby Conjunction, are you?" Linda finally asked.

She ran right across to the giant mushroom.

75

"Yes," replied the tiny thing, lisping prettily and still clinging tightly to her mushroom.

"Now look here," said Barry, trying to speak to a baby as a baby should be spoken to, yet feeling very hazy as to how one went about such things, "you mustn't be scared of us, you know, 'cause we're your pals, and—and we just want to know all about you."

"For instance," Linda brought in, "what do you do with yourself all day long, little Conjunction? Are you very busy, the same as the other Parts of Speech?"

"Yes, ever and ever so busy," the tiny girl answered, now seeming far less shy and really anxious to talk, for once she had got over being frightened she could talk as well as anybody.

That is one of the big differences between Grammar babies and mortal ones, that no matter how young or small they may be, Grammar ones can always find plenty to talk about.

"And just how do you keep busy?" asked Linda.

"Holding hands with things and connecting them." she said.

"Things? What sort of things?" asked Barry. "Words?"

"Yes."

"And anything else?" asked Linda.

"Yes. Often I hold hands with sentences also, and clauses and phrases."

"Well, that's a nice useful thing to be doing

"Holding hands with things."

76

isn't it?" said Barry, but he said that more to be pleasant than because he really thought so.

"Yes," she answered eagerly, "it is, it is, 'cause if I didn't connect them they'd just be all over the place, and humans wouldn't be able to make anything of them."

"Wouldn't they?" asked Linda not quite seeing why they shouldn't be able to.

"Well," the little lass replied, "if you said 'I, you, he are listening', do you think anybody could be quite sure of what you meant?"

"No, I do not."

"If you didn't know about me, then, you'd find it very hard to say what you wanted to, and it would take you and awful time, 'cause you'd have to say something like, 'I am listening, you are listening, he is listening'."

"My word, that would be the worst ever," said Barry.

"Yes, but as you do know about me," she continued, "you can say, 'I, you and he are listening', and everything is all right."

"Well, well, that's wonderful," said Barry, smiling broadly. "And here was I always taking little words like 'and' for granted, and never thinking of them as real, live Parts of Speech."

Opened her eyes wide with surprise.

The Little Grammar People

At this Baby Conjunction opened her eyes wide with surprise. "Oh," she said, "but it's just little words like that that are the most important of all, 'cause they're the ones that make your language smooth and graceful."

"Goodness me, but how?" asked Linda, thinking how funny it was to hear such a tiny girl saying such wise and mysterious things.

"Well, you see," she explained, "everything looks nicer when it's linked up together and flowing smoothly than it does when it's all fallen to pieces and each piece has to jerk along for itself. And if it weren't for me, I don't like to imagine what might happen to King Speech when he goes out walking."

"King Speech!" Barry repeated, looking very much impressed. "Are you really on walking terms with him, little Conjunction?"

And now the tiny girl lifted out the hem of her frock to its full width, which was just her way of looking as proud and important as Small Boy Preposition had done when he thrust his hands into his pockets. "Why," she answered, "King Speech says I'm one of his very favourite little handmaidens—"

"Handmaidens?" said Linda.

"Yes, 'cause I keep holding his hand and showing him the easiest and smoothest way through all the nasty rocky parts. And he often says that if I didn't help him out like that his elegance would quite fall to pieces and he'd have to go bumping along with Old Man Full-stop right at his heels, and with all sorts of jerks and jolts and hops and bounces instead of nice, slow, dignified and kingly steps."

"My, oh my!" Barry exclaimed, and he and Linda felt suddenly so awed

"He might even get tired of himself."

78

that for a few seconds they could think of nothing to say. Then at last, Linda murmured thoughtfully,

"Yes, of course. And if we didn't know you, it would be just as hard for us to join up whole phrases as it would be to join up separate words, wouldn't it? We'd have to use Old Man Full-stop so much that every one would get tired of him, and—and he might even get tired of himself, too."

"Yes, yes, he would, he would!" the tiny girl exclaimed excitedly, clapping her chubby hands and laughing.

"But," Linda continued, "you can be lots of other words as well as 'and', can't you, little Conjunction?"

"Yes, lots and lots and lots," she answered merrily. " 'And' only tells you that something is being added—the same as 'also', 'too' and 'moreover'. But I can also tell you that one thing has been caused by some other thing, and so humans would say that I connected them as 'cause and effect'."

"Goodness me," said Barry, "that sounds hard, and you—you're such a little thing. However do you do it?"

"Simply by being words like 'therefore', 'so' and 'thus'."

"Oh. I see," Barry replied. " 'Mary lost her shoe, so she looked for it everywhere.' Is that right?"

"Yes. And I can connect things by choice, too."

"What on earth does that mean?" asked Linda.

"Well, if you say, 'I must buy either this vase or that one', you can see that I'm connecting this vase and that one by 'either' and 'or', can't you?"

"Oh yes, of course. And you'd be connecting them by choice because that sentence means that I'd have to *choose* between them. Oh, it's all easy, easy. And, little Conjunction, how else do you connect things?"

"Well, sometimes by having very much my own idea about them, and holding on to this no matter what anybody says, so that I can, for instance, say that something *can* happen in spite of something else, no matter how much it may seem that it can't."

"Dear me, that sounds very complicated indeed," Barry exclaimed.

"It isn't really, though," she assured him, "for when you say, 'It was raining hard, *but* she went to see them', you mean that she was able to go and see them *in spite of* the fact that it was raining hard."

"Of course, of course," he cried, annoyed with himself for not having understood immediately. "And the same with words like 'however' and 'yet'. Please, little Conjunction, do go on. What other words can you be?"

"Well, I'm lots and lots of others—too many to tell you of just now. But sometimes I get awfully uncertain about things—simply can't make up my mind—and then I am words like 'if' and 'unless'."

"Yes, I see," said Linda. "And so you connect things together in doubt, don't you? For instance, when I used to say, 'I'm sure I could do grammar *if* I saw any sense in it', you used to be in my sentence as 'if', connecting 'I'm sure I could do grammar' with 'I saw any sense in it.' Oh, whatever would we mortals do without you, little Conjunction?"

"I don't know," the tiny girl answered seriously. "I don't really know." And then, after a short pause, she added, "Sometimes I compare—"

"Oh," said Barry. showing off what he knew, "like Madam Adjective."

"No, no, not a bit like her," came the quick reply, "for when you say 'I like this more than that', you are comparing, aren't you?—comparing 'this' and 'that'."

"Yes."

"Well, in that sentence I am 'than'."

Wee Baby Conjunction

"Oh, I see," said Linda. "And when you're comparing, you could also be 'as', couldn't you?"

"Yes, and other words, too. So altogether, do you really think you'll know me from now on, when you meet me in sentences?"

"Know you!" Barry exclaimed.

"Why, we couldn't possibly help it, little Conjunction," Linda assured her, "no matter how hard we tried not to."

"And you'll never call me a preposition again?"

"Never, never," said Linda.

"We can promise you that," Barry added.

And then, after smiling shyly at both the children and at Sir Desire, the baby girl edged round to the back of her mushroom and toddled away as fast as she could go. But as she went, she sang a funny little song to herself which Barry and Linda liked so much that, acting on Sir Desire's advice, they learned it off by heart, just to make quite sure of recognizing Wee Baby Conjunction whenever they should meet her again right through their lives. And these were the words of her song:

> Remember, mortals, when you see
> Me adding things, I'll be to you
> Perhaps 'moreover', 'and', or 'too'.
> And when with causes and effects
> I play awhile, it's then, you know,
> I'm words like 'thus', 'because', and 'so'.
> And when I choose 'tween several things
> You'll recognize me, I am sure,
> In little words like 'either', 'or'.
> At times I find myself in doubt.
> Then I become—well, can you guess?
> Simply 'providing', 'if', 'unless'.

The Little Grammar People

Or I may say some things *can* be
In spite of others. Don't forget
Little 'however', 'but', and 'yet'.
And when I help you to compare,
As, mortal friends, I often can
It's then I'm words like 'as' and 'than'.

CHAPTER XII

THE POOR LETTERS

THE two children and Sir Desire all sat down on the grass under a shady tree to have a little rest. Sir Desire seemed suddenly to have grown sleepy and, try as they would, both Linda and Barry felt as if they simply could not hold their eyes open.

And now it was that they saw one of the prettiest things possible to dreams or magic—thousands of fairies all dressed in long, dark, misty blue gowns, flying across the sky like a flock of silent birds, and carrying with them a huge, billowy curtain the same colour as their gowns. From one end of the sky to the other they flew with their precious burden until the sunshine was quite blotted out, and night was spread over the Kingdom of Grammar in deep, rich folds.

Then suddenly, from all directions, millions upon millions of large fireflies arose, and flew up, up, up, higher and higher until at last they reached the beautiful dark curtain; and, scattering themselves all over this, they clung to it as tightly as they could.

"There are the stars," said Linda, trying in vain to make Sir Desire believe she was wide awake.

"Yes," he answered in a slow, dreamy voice, "there are the stars."

And when Linda next looked at him, she saw by starlight that he was fast asleep.

Next morning Barry was the first to wake up and, glancing at the sky, he quickly nudged his sister. "Linda, wake up! Look!" he whispered in her ear.

Instantly Linda started up, and she almost cried aloud with wonder and surprise, for she was just in time to see a throng of the loveliest fairies all dressed in pale pink frocks, flying across the sky the opposite way to that chosen by the night fairies. Each of them was holding a tiny scrap of that dark curtain to which the firefly stars had clung throughout the night, and in this way it was carefully being carried back into the Castle of Shadow, which was where it rested all day long, with the whole company of night fairies fluttering a soft-winged guard over it. And finally, when the dawn fairies had tucked away every particle of that precious mantle, a golden, laughing sun popped out and spilt a few beams down into the Kingdom of Grammar, and it was day.

"Oh," cried Linda, "how lovely, lovely!"

"My word!" said Barry. "It was bonzer all right. Wish we could have things like that back home, Lin."

"Perhaps we have," said Linda thoughtfully, "but just don't happen to see as clearly as—as we do here "

"Yes, you know, there's something in that. Barry answered, also thoughtfully.

"Oh, but I wonder—I do wonder—what'll be happening to us to-day!" Linda suddenly exclaimed. "I can't wait to know—I can't, I can't!"

Immediately there was a sharp rustling sound in the grass, and Sir Desire was awake. Up he sprang, exactly like a jack-in-the-box, with a broad, happy laugh all over him.

"Good gracious, I'm so excited I can hardly keep

Turning a few somersaults.

still," he cried, turning a few somersaults and then standing on his head for fully five minutes—or so it seemed—while he pondered as to where he would first take Barry and Linda, for he considered that his best thinking position.

However, he had not as yet made up his mind by a long way when an agitated movement started up amongst a few of the bushes that surrounded the garden. Sir Desire quickly got down on to his feet and, with the children, watched this curiously for a few seconds, when from the very middle of it there appeared an extremely hot and bothered little old man wearing a long black gown and hurrying towards them for all he was worth.

"Why," said Barry, "it's the good old judge, who was so upset about those H's I—"

"Yes, yes," came the puffed-out reply, "but I'm a thousand times more upset now, I can tell you."

"Dear me, whatever for?" asked Linda. "Whatever has happened, Mr Judge?"

"You should come to the Court and see," he answered, with tears in his voice. "It's—it's in an uproar—a perfect uproar. I—I just want to sit down and weep when I see my dear, sweet, precious Court in such a hullabaloo."

"But tell us, Mr Judge," said Barry, looking distressed, "what's gone wrong?"

"Ah!" he sighed. Then he was silent for a long while, after which he sighed again and actually did wipe a few tears away with his tiny pocket handkerchief. Then, having given a few more sighs in double quick time, he continued, "You see, although we are beginning another day by fairy time, children are still on their way home from school by mortal time, and—and they're dropping absolutely everything. I think they do it deliberately—I really do. Sometimes I fear there'll never be an end to this—this horrible carelessness."

"Are they," Barry ventured to ask, "dropping H's, Mr Judge?"

"H's? Why, they're dropping everything they *can* drop. Yes, yes, H's are, of course, amongst the poor discarded goods, together with dozens of Th's and hundreds of G's. Oh dear, oh dear, what shall I do?"

Linda was so upset by the little judge's wailings that she took his hand and patted it gently. "Come along," she said, "we'll all go to the Court with you and see what we can do."

He seemed relieved at this, but every now and then during the journey Linda and Barry each had to take hold of one of his hands and drag him along by main force, as he would stop abruptly and, calling out "I can't bear to look at it! No, no, I can't bear it!" would refuse to go any farther.

When finally they did arrive at the Grammar Court, however, it was clear that he had not exaggerated his misfortunes, for everything appeared to be quite out of hand, and the little judge, taking the merest glance at it all, uttered one long howl.

For a short time the two children and Sir Desire looked on in silence. Sir Desire was very much inclined to giggle at the absurd positions that some of the letters were getting themselves into, but Linda and Barry remained very solemn.

Although there were not many K's or P's in that odd

The poor letters.

assembly, there were a few, and all of them seemed to be crippled. A good many H's and G's were, too. The children thought this very strange, and when they saw that the judge had grown quieter, Barry asked him why they should be.

"It's very sad to look upon," he replied mournfully. "For all the upheaval and the numbers of wounded you really would think my dear Court was a battle-field. But yes, I'll tell you the reason for these poor letters being crippled. H's, as you see, are dropped unmercifully. Constant pleas are being sent out to pick them up, but instead of making the situation better they only make it worse."

"Oh, but why?" asked Linda.

"Because there are many cruel, thoughtless people in the world who, upon hearing these pleas, only want to mock them. So they do pick up the H's, but attach them to words where they do not and cannot belong. How many times has a poor H been attached to the beginnings of words like 'after', 'altogether', 'interior', 'odour', 'oven', 'eternal'! Ah me, ah me! And then, of course, being so out of place and thrown out of gear, the poor H becomes crippled."

"The poor H!" repeated Linda and Barry together.

"And what about the poor K's?" asked Barry.

"Ah, the poor K's! How often does a G get dropped from a word and a K picked up in its stead! How many times does 'thing' become 'think' when it is still supposed to be 'thing', all because a poor K has been evilly picked up out of place and maimed!"

"And," continued Linda with a mournful expression, "what about the poor G's?"

"Ah, the poor G's!" exclaimed the little judge. "Dropped from their rightful stations and picked up in their wrong ones! Dropped out of 'pining' and picked up in 'pincushion'!"

"In 'pincushion'?"

"Yes, yes, making 'pingcushion'."

"Oh," said Barry, "how worrying, Mr Judge! And what about the poor P's?"

"Ah, the poor P's! How many times has a poor P been attached to the word 'something', forming that unspeakable concoction 'sompthing' !"

There seemed nothing else to say, so no one said anything, but every one, except Sir Desire, looked miserable. He, the merry-hearted little imp, kept stuffing chuckles, one after another, up his sleeve—which was bad enough—or swallowing them—which was worse, for then they slipped straight down to his feet and set up all sorts of extraordinary jigs there. Learned as he was, the little judge could find no satisfactory explanation for these, and, with the children, turned woebegone eyes back upon the poor jostling letters. And as he watched, more and more G's and H's came tumbling down into the Court, and more and more began hobbling about in an awkward, crippled manner.

Then came down a whole shower of Th's. And these had no sooner landed than they started rushing here, there and everywhere in the most boisterous and abandoned fashion.

"Dearie me!" whined the little judge. "There's a certain boy at your school, Barry, who is always dropping his poor Th's."

"That must be Murray Wilks," Barry whispered to Linda. "He always says ' 'em' instead of 'them'."

And another Th tumbled down into the riotous Court.

Every second the confusion was growing worse and worse, until the little judge could really bear to look at it no longer.

"Never mind!" Barry said comfortingly. "I'll tell you what we'll do, Mr Judge. We'll set to work straight away and pick all these letters up. We won't leave a single one out. Then we'll call an assembly of all the words they've been dropped from or to which they've been joined unlawfully, and everything'll be fixed up in a twink."

The little judge seemed to approve of this idea wholeheartedly, for his eyes brightened until they sparkled, and he clapped his hands until they ached.

"Good boy, good boy!" he cried. "You're a true friend, Barry—and Linda, you are too—and of course your Sir Desire is too. Come now, come! It's an awful lot to do, and unless we get a move on, we'll still be at it this time next week.

CHAPTER XIII

MESSRS SUBJECT AND PREDICATE

SO they set to work immediately, with the result that only about half the day had gone when at last every one of the wronged letters had been attended to. All that had been dropped were restored to their rightful words, while those which had been crippled by being forced into wrong positions were soon relieved of their slings, crutches and walking-sticks.

"Ha!" cried the little judge merrily. "Now every word is happy, every letter is happy, my Court is in beautiful order, and *I* am happy. Order! Order!" he shouted. "Order in the Court!"

Linda turned to Sir Desire. "But there *is* order in the Court," she whispered. "so why do you think Mr Judge is still asking for it?"

"He says that by force of habit, my dear," replied the tiny man. "Whenever he is particularly pleased about something, or, while a session is being held, suddenly thinks of a brilliant idea, he always shouts at the top of his voice, 'Order in the Court!' "

"I see," said Linda.

The little judge now told the children in as few words as possible that he was most grateful to them but would have to be leaving them, as he was deeply involved in the records of some very ancient and interesting trials. As a matter of fact, they were a few Dative, Genitive and Accusative cases, whose irregularities had long ago been tried in the Latin Grammar Court.

"Poor Mr Judge," said Sir Desire, when he and the children were once more left alone, "if he isn't being worried by the subjects of Grammar Kingdom, those of the mortal world can certainly give him a lot to think about."

"The subjects and predicates?" asked Linda.

"Ha, ha, ha!" laughed the little man. "No, no, no! Ha, ha, ha! But that's a good hint, Lin. For the moment I'd forgotten all about Messrs Subject and Predicate. I couldn't let you go home again without meeting them—"

"But," Barry interrupted, "Master Verb told us that his subject was either Miss Noun, Sir Pronoun or a short phrase."

"Yes, Barry. But supposing you wanted to ask Subject a question, it would be rather awkward to have to interview Miss Noun, Sir Pronoun and a short phrase, don't you think?"

"Yes, I s'pose so."

"Well, it's for that very reason that Mr Subject has become a citizen of Grammar Kingdom—to represent these three. It's so much easier to speak with one person than with three about the same thing."

"Yes, of course it is," Linda agreed.

"Well, then," Sir Desire concluded, "come and we'll see if we can find him. The subject of a sentence is a most important person, you know."

"Subject of a sentence!" Barry repeated, looking puzzled. "But I thought it was only Master Verb who had a subject."

"Yes, but you've forgotten, Barry, that a sentence can only be a sentence if Master Verb is in it. And if he isn't in it—well, it's just something else."

"What else?" asked Linda.

"Well, a phrase, to be exact," the little man replied.

"Oh, I see."

"So, of course, Master Verb's subject is also the sentence's subject."

"Hm, quite a saving!" Barry observed.

And then, without any more ado, the little trio set out from the Court in search of this "most important person". Climbing through the fence, they found themselves on the top of a steep slope covered with thick, soft grass.

"Let's take hands and run to the bottom," said Linda.

"No, let's roll," said Barry.

"Oh, yes!" agreed Linda and Sir Desire.

So they all lay down on the top of the slope and rolled down, down, down to the very bottom, laughing and shouting with every turn, and arriving very giddy indeed. But when at last they stood up to see where they were, they noticed two funny little gnome-like men quite close to them.

"Well, well, well," said Sir Desire, "this *is* a lucky meeting. Lin and Barry, this is Mr Subject, and—"

"And," continued Mr Subject, pointing down at his companion gnome, who was sitting on the grass, "this is Mr Predicate. We are quite indispensable to one another, you know."

"Yes," said Barry, "that's the trouble, isn't it?"

"Trouble? Not at all. It's the easiest thing in the world."

"Oh, but I mean trouble for me and Lin," Barry hastened to explain.

"You see, at school you are always spoken of

"We are quite indispensable to one another."

together—and it isn't fair, because even when I can pick one of you out in a sentence my answer isn't any good unless I can pick the other one out too."

"Yes, that's right," Linda agreed. "I can mostly find you fairly easily, Mr Subject, but your friend Mr Predicate is always playing hide-and-seek."

"Hide-and-seek?" repeated Mr Subject, shaking all over with laughter.

"Yes, he hides and I seek. But he knows all the hard places, so I never find him. And Miss Randal says that you, Mr Subject, are simply no good without him."

"Indeed!" replied the little gnome, letting the corners of his mouth curve down into the funniest pout.

"That's right, that's right!" cried Mr Predicate, jumping to his feet and looking very pleased with himself. "And I'll tell you why, too. My friend Mr Subject is one of those people who must be talked about continually; and if he isn't being talked about he becomes so insignificant that you don't notice him, and soon you just about forget that he even exists. Now, as I am kind enough to do all the talking he requires, and as no one else in Grammar Kingdom could serve his purpose as well as I do, I am the one who must be given all the credit for keeping him in your mind."

"I see," said Linda.

"So, that's why Miss Randal says he's no good without me, because—well, simply because he isn't, I suppose."

"On the other hand." Mr Subject quickly added, "my dear friend Mr Predicate is such a perpetual talker that if he had nothing to talk about he'd still keep on chattering—about that—and would make himself completely ridiculous. Now, as I am kind enough to provide, in myself, all the 'subject' matter he requires, and as no one else in Grammar Kingdom could serve his purpose as well as I do, I am the one who must be given all the credit for keeping his reputation unharmed."

"My reputation!" exclaimed the Predicate gnome.

"Yes, of being even faintly sensible."

"Well then, it seems to me," said Barry, "that you should both be awfully glad to have each other."

"And that's exactly what we are!" they cried out together.

"Yes, 'cause you're both very good to one another," said Linda.

"Not always, by any means," Mr Subject contradicted.

"Often Mr Predicate says things about me that I don't a bit like—that are anything but pleasing, in fact."

"And often," added Mr Predicate. "Mr Subject chooses to be things that I simply hate talking about, yet I have to talk about them just the same."

They had a round of good hearty laughter at that, then Barry asked the Predicate gnome,

"And do you always say a lot about Mr Subject?"

"No, no. Sometimes I've only got a single word to say, so that's all I do say." He hesitated for a minute, and then asked mischievously, "I wonder if either of you could tell me what Part of Speech that single word would have to be?"

And as, after a great deal of thought, the twins were both very sorry but could make no really good suggestion,

"Why," he exclaimed, "it could be none other than Master Verb, for he simply has to appear at least once in whatever I say, so if I only say one word—"

"Oh yes, of course—that word must be Master Verb," Linda said eagerly.

"Quite so," answered the two gnomes, speaking on top of one another.

"So that in the sentence 'The monkey climbs', you are 'monkey', aren't you, Mr Subject?" asked Barry.

"Yes, yes—although I hate to admit it," replied the little man.

"And 'climbs' is the only thing said about you. Now, because it is said about you it is Mr Predicate, and because it is only one word it must be Master Verb—and it is Master Verb."

"Right!" shouted Sir Desire.

"Right!" agreed the two gnomes.

"Say, Lin," cried Mr Predicate, his eyes goggling with mischief, "are we still playing hide-and-seek, you and I?"

"Oh no," she answered gaily. "Now that I've found you at last, I'll never mislay you again."

CHAPTER XIV

KING SPEECH

"YOU'LL soon have to be going home again, children," said Sir Desire, "and I'll miss you a lot."

"Yes, we'll miss you too," said Linda. "Although," she added after a pause, "you are our own true desire to learn and understand things, and as we'll always be keeping that, won't we always be keeping you—just as we can see you now?"

"Yes, that's right," Barry agreed. "You'll never leave us, Sir Desire, Lin and I won't let you."

The little man looked up at the two children gratefully. "As long as you truly want me," he said, "I'll be with you, sure as sure. But what I mean is that perhaps you'll never actually see me again, for, although you may not have thought it, there are very, very few mortals who have ever visited Grammar Kingdom and met its little people the way you have. Any amount may desire, but only a few can see."

"Why?" asked Barry.

"Because only those people who are lucky enough to have a fairy in their hearts can see."

"Oh, does that really mean, then," Linda asked, her voice trembling with excitement, "that Barry and I have a fairy in our hearts?"

"Yes, you must have. Otherwise you'd be able to read sentences only as they're written down in books, and recognize Parts of Speech only by their names and definitions. Yet in

96

reality names and definitions are nothing more than empty shells, which have no life in them and no beauty. They can be seen and heard just any old time by your mortal eyes and ears, but it's the fairy in your hearts who sees their happy little souls and hears their sweet voices.

"And there are very few mortals—yes, very, very few—who would believe the things that a fairy in their hearts could show them. They little know that mortal ears are deaf and mortal eyes are blind. And so, to all those million things that they cannot understand they give such names as 'dreams', 'fancies', 'imaginations', and 'common fibs'. But by doing this they're only building around themselves a hard, cruel wall of unbelief which, although they think it a defence, is really a prison."

And now, for the first time, the little man looked so sad and serious that Barry and Linda felt quite sorry for him.

"But," said Linda, "we—Barry and I—we'll always keep our fairy, won't we, Sir Desire?"

Still looking wistful and after hesitating a moment, "I wonder," he replied.

Then suddenly and quite unexpectedly, he burst into a peal of joyous laughter. "Come, come!" he cried. "We're wasting time. We only have a little while longer, so we mustn't be sad in it."

And with this, taking Barry's hand in one of his and Linda's in the other, he ran forward for all he was worth.

"Oh, Sir Desire, whatever's happening? Where are we off to now?" shouted the twins.

"You'll see in a few minutes." he shouted back.

And they kept on running like a family of scampering rabbits until all of a sudden they found themselves in the heart of a dense, dark forest. Barry and Linda had never before seen trees so straight and tall. Every one of them seemed to be

A dense dark forest.

stretching up and trying to touch the sky with the tips of its tallest branches; and they certainly interfered with the sun, for in the whole forest there was never a sign of his golden beams.

Here the three travellers stopped a minute while their breaths caught up with them, and as their eyes grew more accustomed to the darkness Barry and Linda saw, extending from where they were right on into the distance, a long, ribbon-like pathway, winding and narrow.

Then on and on down this pathway they walked, their feet and legs growing tired, and wondering all the time what they would be finding at the end of their long journey. It was useless asking Sir Desire, for that wee fellow utterly refused to give any answer except a soft chuckle and a mysterious "You'll see!" And it seemed, as the minutes kept on passing by, that the winding path would never finish. But of course, finally it did.

All of a sudden and when it was least expected to, it opened out into a tremendous circular space, surrounded by what seemed to be simply thousands of trees even taller than any the children had yet seen. And way up in the air, their great spreading branches had grown in from all directions towards the centre, carrying on them the thickest coats of leaves.

Dainty, thin-stalked creepers, which had twined themselves around the trunk of each separate tree until they had reached the top, now looped themselves across and across in every possible direction, so that they drooped down from the towering roof like a rich tapestry of cobwebs. And, stationed all over them without leaving a single pin-point uncovered, were millions upon millions of fireflies and glow-worms, who filled the whole of that wonderful palace with a gentle, fairy-like radiance.

The Little Grammar People

The ground was as soft as swansdown to walk on, and the awe-inspired children, looking down at it, saw that they were standing on a thick carpet of emerald-coloured moss.

But amid all this magic beauty, nothing was quite as lovely as the two graceful thrones which stood side by side at the head of the palace and were made entirely of dewdrops.

Every morning when the sun first awakes, you will have noticed, dear Reader, how he fills each dewdrop in the garden with a shimmering, many-coloured light. Now the fairies, watching their opportunity, had gathered these shining drops at that very second when they were brightest, and had waved a spell over them so that they would never fade or perish. Then they had carried them to the tree palace, handfuls at a time, and had carefully built them up there into the forms of two sparkling thrones, where they looked exactly like a treasure house of liquid opals.

On one throne sat the loveliest white-haired and white-bearded old man imaginable who, when he stood up, was very tall. On the other throne sat a lady so sweetly beautiful as to appear like some dream of enchantment almost too delicate to look upon.

The loveliest white-haired old man.

Then Barry and Linda noticed that the snowy-haired old man—King Speech himself—was standing erect and majestically, and that, with the gentlest smile on his face, he was speaking to them.

"Welcome to my kingdom, little mortal, children. My old heart is indeed filled with joy that you have come here before returning to your home. Few visitors ever come to me from the mortal world—few and scattered: at times separated from one another by hundreds of years—since they are only those few who are able to believe in the life of so-called 'lifeless' things."

Neither Barry nor Linda could say a single word. They both opened their mouths to speak, but no sound would come.

Once again Linda turned her eyes upon that indescribable lady dressed all in purest white and she could not imagine why, but suddenly she felt two large, warm tears trickling down her cheeks.

The old man noticed this and, taking the lady's shell-like hand, he said, "This, Linda, is my queen. She has a name that I think you will always remember, as it is one of the most beautiful words in the whole wide world. Her name is Poetry.

"Her name is
Poetry."

"Ah yes. you can see her now—you and Barry—and you can admire her, for her face is very, very lovely, and her voice is the sweetest in all the world; but as yet you may not understand all of her. True it is that you have learnt and are masters of many things. But true also is it that as yet you may still be wrapped about in the silken cocoon of childhood. And for some of you that is something very protective and very sweet, but also dense. No, my friends, years may have to pass, and Life will have to show you many of his deepest joys and sorrows, before you will understand more of the mysteries of this beautiful lady's soul, for she is at once gentle and as wild as the storm spirit, happy and infinitely sad, relentless and full of compassion; she can dance with elves and fairies on cobwebs and moonbeams, and can also march through battle-fields with fierce war drums beating in her heart. But always she is warm and living. In other words, she is the soul of vast humanity. And when, in years to come, you break free from those silken childhood cocoons, and spread your wings to fly bravely into the hot sunshine of human feeling, you will come to better know my queen. Then you may even feel able to speak with her heart to heart."

Again Linda tried to say something, but could not. She looked down at Sir Desire, and saw that he was smiling at her with the tenderest light in his eyes she had ever seen. Barry looked down at him too at this moment, and the tiny being also smiled at him. Afterwards, the children realized that this had been his way of saying good-bye.

Suddenly the palace had disappeared with all its magnificence, Sir Desire had disappeared, Grammar Kingdom had disappeared; and there were Barry and Linda sitting side by side on the banks of their own little woodland creek which, had it entered their minds a moment before, they would have thought to be hundreds and thousands of miles away.

Instantly they both looked for their old friend the obstinate leaf. And yes, there it was, still caught against the little clump of reeds. But at that moment, for no apparent reason, it jerked away, and drifted down, with the water current, out of sight.

CHAPTER XV

HOME

THAT night before going to bed, Barry and Linda crept up to one of the windows in their mortal home and looked towards the gully they had always loved so well. Now, it had an added meaning for them, and an added charm. They felt that they would always think of it with a certain awe as well as with their usual fondness—and they always did.

Also, of course, they felt as if they would love to tell the whole world about their wonderful adventures in the Kingdom of Grammar; but they knew all too well how unbelieving their schoolmates would be, and not for anything would they allow the dear little Grammar people to suffer such scorn. So they satisfied themselves by telling their mother and father only, and the next day after school they told Miss Randal.

But even to this very day Barry and Linda are often known to steal away by themselves and talk softly together, sometimes for more than an hour on end. And no one can hear a word of what they are saying, but their mother and father, who love and understand them, know quite well that they are talking once again on their favourite of all topics—about certain little people whose names were Miss Noun, Sir Pronoun, Madam Adjective, Master Verb, Lady Adverb, Small Boy Preposition, Interjection Esquire, and Wee Baby Conjunction, and about that most lovable and inseparable pair of friends Messrs Subject and Predicate. And sometimes also, though rather more seldom and with even softer voices, they whisper their memories of that beautiful, firefly-lighted palace where lived the fairy-like Queen Poetry and her snowy-haired King Speech.

ALSO BY NURI MASS

MAGIC AUSTRALIA

By
NURI MASS

Decorated By
CELESTE MASS

For more living books from this author and many others please visit our website-

WWW.LIVINGBOOKPRESS.COM